Praise for Unlocking Private Company Wealth

Chris' latest book, *Unlocking Private Company Wealth,* is an absolute "must read" for all business owners. It digs deep into the "illiquid" wealth locked up in most successful businesses and provides great strategies on how to ultimately unlock that wealth. Chris' 25 questions on managing private wealth will not only get you thinking, it should cause you to take action!

Allan D. Koltin
Chief Executive Officer, Koltin Consulting Group
Chicago, Illinois

Prescient, practical, down to earth tools for privately held companies. I've witnessed Chris in action in the boardroom using these very ideas. The concepts matter in *Unlocking Private Company Wealth,* and Chris can build value for you with them. Read the book.

Dennis Allen
Chief Executive Officer, Jones Stephens
Birmingham, Alabama

Decades of my own experience with private business owners tell me this book will be an eye-opener for many. *Unlocking Private Company Wealth* will be valuable for both those owners who expect to sell the entire business at some point down the road and for those who have no intention of ever selling. Mercer demonstrates the need for managing not only the business but the ownership of it – as an asset that dominates the financial well-being of the owners and their families. Then he explains in clear language how the tools of financial management can be used to respond to that need.

Don Kozusko
Managing Partner, Kozusko Harris Duncan
Washington, D.C.

Unlocking Private Company Wealth reviews many of the issues we have been dealing with in succession planning for our company. It lays out much of what we have discussed with professionals. This work is a call to action on developing and executing a plan and lays out the options to move forward.

Russ Stigge
Chief Executive Officer, Plains Equipment Group
Lincoln, Nebraska

Unlocking Private Company Wealth is a practical guide to managing and unlocking private company wealth. Mercer's insights challenge the reader to re-think how you view ownership in a privately held company. The book is a must read for business owners and their advisors!

Martin Willoughby
Principal, Butler Snow Advisory Services
Memphis, Tennessee
Author, Zoom Entrepreneur

If you're a sophisticated business owner or advisor to business owners, you need to read and implement suggestions in *Unlocking Private Company Wealth*. Think about this book as a survey course on how to manage the investment known as your business. If you gave half the attention to learning Mercer's strategies and techniques as you do with your liquid investments, you would have a much happier financial outcome when it's time to leave your business. Here are some questions for you to ponder that are answered in the book:

1. Do you pay regular dividends and do you have a strategy for managing them?

2. Do you have a method for understanding what the value of your company is?

3. How are you managing risk within your business?

4. Do you think about your business as one that is an investment as well as one that provides income?

5. If you were an outside investor, would you want to own your business?

Unlocking Private Company Wealth will help you answer these questions. It will force you to look at your business as a wealth creation tool. You get to understand what drives private company wealth, as well as great methods of managing that wealth. Advisors need to understand the principles presented in this book. You'll find that you'll have more intelligent conversations with your clients and you'll be able to help your clients make wise decisions. I hope you take the time to read and understand Mercer's message. Business owners and advisors will benefit from the effort.

Josh Patrick
Founding Principal, Stage 2 Planning Partners
South Burlington, Vermont
New York Times Blogger

In an environment where blogs and blasts partially describe a lot – and thoroughly detail nothing – Chris Mercer stands out as an exception. *Unlocking Private Company Wealth* captures the essence of unlocking the wealth and capital inside a privately held business. From valuation and liquidity issues to the arcane world of legal structures, Chris provides a flexible road map for business owners and advisors – a road map that helps successfully manage wealth.

The challenge to providing ideas for unlocking wealth in a privately held business is the topic's breadth and complexity. Chris Mercer's book cuts through the clutter and provides a clear and cogent view of how to create, monetize, manage and transfer capital.

When a business owner seeks to unlock the wealth of a business, the challenge is the army of advisors that must be deployed. Chris Mercer's book consolidates the information on two issues, challenges and opportunities in monetizing business wealth, and serves it up in a clear and readable fashion.

Steve Parrish, JD, CLU, ChFC, RHU
National Advanced Solutions Director, Principal Financial Group
Des Moines, Iowa
Contributor, Forbes.com

It's best to take action when the circumstances are favorable and the timing is right. *Unlocking Private Company Wealth* examines strategies you can implement now that will increase the future value of your closely held business.

Bill Rankin, CPA
Chief Financial Officer, Blue Bell Creameries, LP
Brenham, Texas

I used to think it was odd how business owners would closely monitor the performance of a few hundred thousand dollars in a retirement account, but have no idea how many millions their business was worth. Stranger still was the fact that their financial advisors didn't seem to recognize this as a problem. *Unlocking Private Company Wealth* illuminates this lopsided view of wealth management and offers a number of smart solutions to fit any business/owner situation. This book is a must-read for business owners and their advisors. Not reading it – or taking Chris Mercer's wisdom to heart – is leaving money on the table. *Unlocking Private Company Wealth* brings clear perspective and concrete solutions to one of the missing pieces of business ownership – how to turn a lifetime of work into a legacy of wealth.

Barbara Taylor, MBA

Co-Founder, Allan Taylor & Company
Rogers, Arkansas
New York Times Blogger

I have been in and around privately held family businesses for over 40 years. I believe every family member owner, especially those who don't work in their family's business, needs to read Chris' book. It is an excellent framework for understanding the importance of their investment and provides essential concepts to assist them in understanding and measuring for themselves the value of what is, for most, the largest asset in their investment portfolio. I plan on sharing it with our Family Council as a great educational tool for our family owners.

Daniel B. Hatzenbuehler

Chairman of the Board, E. Ritter & Company
Marked Tree, Arkansas

Unlocking Private Company Wealth is packed full of outstanding information and valuable advice for anyone who owns or is considering purchasing or investing in a privately held company. Not only does this book share key ways to preserve existing wealth, but also ideas for how to grow that value. Chris Mercer has a way of simplifying very complex transactions. Thank you for sharing your insights, Chris, and making all private companies better.

Emily Nielsen
Corporate Treasurer, Gallup
Omaha, Nebraska

True to form, Chris has delivered an erudite action plan for any stakeholder in the value of a private company. If you have before resolved to change the status quo and finally – focus on what you need to do to drive growth, Unlocking Private Company Wealth will motivate you to get serious about enhancing and monitoring financial performance. Chris clearly and cogently outlines various options and concrete strategies. His tactical approaches like *The One Percent Solution,* the implementation of a dividend policy, consideration of minority interest private equity investment and the READY (Risks, Earnings, Attitudes/Aptitudes/Actions, Driving Growth, Year to Year Comparisons) framework will form the basis of the business plan you won't want to put off any longer. Readers of this book will be lucky indeed to count Chris in their circle of outside advisors whose counsel is essential for taking a business to the next level.

Lucretia Lyons
President, Business Valuation Resources, LLC
Portland, Oregon

As the fourth-generation CEO of a family business, I can assure you that the concepts Chris introduces with his *One Percent Solution* idea – making deliberate investments in such things as estate planning, outside board members, and annual stock valuations – are critical to success if you wish to perpetuate your business to future generations. One percent may not be the right number for everyone, but we would not still be here today as a family business if our previous generations of owners had not made those important investments.

David J. Duda
President & Chief Executive Officer, A. Duda & Sons, Inc.
Oviedo, Florida

Too many business owners go to work every day and manage their people, their tasks, even their cash flow, but not enough of them are giving thought to wisely managing their business as an asset. Chris Mercer has no peer when it comes to valuing a business, and offering perspective on managing that asset. Read his new book and you will be inspired by creative possibilities and informed on multiple fronts for managing all opportunities afforded you through your enterprise.

Don Hutson
Chief Executive Officer, U. S. Learning
Memphis, Tennessee
#1 New York Times and Wall Street Journal Best-Selling co-author of
The One Minute Negotiator and Selling Value

Chris has provided a well-organized discussion of the wealth management responsibilities and techniques that owners, executives and managers of private businesses should appreciate. In an easy-to-read style, with real world examples, he covers a variety of topics around the fundamental theme that wealth, separate and apart from the business itself, must be actively managed and stewarded by and for the ownership. Critical to perpetuating businesses for multiple generations is recognition of this fact.

Barton Weeks

Executive Vice President and Chief Operating Officer, A. Duda & Sons, Inc.
Oviedo, Florida

Great book! Two thoughts reverberated in my mind as I was reading it. First, I would have made such better decisions with my own business had I read this book sooner! (And I wish I had) And second, every Financial Advisor who has business owners clients must read this book and help their clients make better decisions about managing their company wealth.

Bill Bachrach

CEO and author of Values-Based Financial Planning
San Diego, California

After owning my business for 25 years, I have always thought of myself as a good, smart business person. Your book, *Unlocking Private Company Wealth* helped me think through so many critical issues relating to the wealth of both my company and my family that I have never addressed or considered creating a plan. This book is a must read for every business owner.

Peter Stark

President, Peter Barron Stark Companies
San Diego, California

I live and work in the world of privately owned (usually family owned) businesses. Chris Mercer's *Unlocking Private Company Wealth* is a breath of fresh air, a systematic and thoughtful way to look at the "wealth" locked in a privately held business with the same dispassion and analytic calm that most owners insist on in the management of their investment portfolios. The emotional ties to and personal relationships within privately held companies frequently result in something akin to "management by intuition", an inherited or habit-formed set of "strategies" that can go unchallenged for decades.

The chapter on "Tools for Private Company Wealth" provides, by itself, a matrix for any business to periodically look at itself not as its insiders see it, but as outsiders would. Armed with that discipline the owners can then make decisions that explicitly acknowledge current market thinking. If the decision is to opt out of "maximizing value" for tactical or personal reasons, then it is done with intentionality. A deliberate decision to forego maximizing short or mid-term "realizable" value for the owners may be grounded in very real and defensible values or strategy, but that grounding is stronger when it recognizes the trade-offs it entails.

At its heart, *Unlocking Private Company Wealth* is a proposal for the opposite of "Management by Intuition." In no way does analysis commit the business to management denuded of values or longer term strategy. Rather it is the Best Practice for a company and its owners to make knowing decisions and allocations of resources.

Stephen G. Salley, JD
Partner, Banyan Family Business Advisors
Orlando, Florida

After decades of advising entrepreneurs on liquid assets, I found this book to be a great tool to help entrepreneurs evaluate their business in the context of all their assets. Chris highlights questions and concepts that help entrepreneurs frame up opportunities and risk holistically.

Steven Sansom
Co-Founder, Green Square Capital
Memphis, Tennessee
YPO-WPO International Board

With this new book, *Unlocking Private Company Wealth*, Chris continues his insightful and very helpful thoughts about important topics for virtually anyone who has involvement with a family business. The concepts he sets forth and suggestions he makes are quite enlightening. This book is a "must read" in particular for members of any family business from generations 1-4.

Spence Wilson
Chairman, Kemmons Wilson Companies
Memphis, Tennessee
Multi-Year Client of the Mercer Companies

Read *Unlocking Private Company Wealth*. The contents will help every reader be able to make better decisions managing business wealth. Advisors will be richer in knowledge and can use the ideas and techniques to help clients become richer in value creation in their businesses and in accumulating wealth independent of their businesses.

Edward Mendlowitz, CPA/ABV, PFS
Partner, Withum Smith & Brown, PC
New Brunswick, New Jersey

Unlocking Private Company Wealth

Proven Strategies and Tools for Managing
Wealth in Your Private Business

Z. Christopher Mercer, ASA, CFA, ABAR

Unlocking
Private Company Wealth

Proven Strategies and Tools for Managing Wealth in Your Private Business

ISBN: 978-0-9700698-8-7

Peabody Publishing LP
5100 Poplar Avenue
Suite 2600
Memphis, Tennessee 38137
901.685.2120 (p)

To my father, Zeno C. Mercer (deceased),
O. Lafayette Walker (deceased), Charlie Andrews,
Ben Bolch, Robert McFarlin,
Robert Rogers (deceased), Ian Arnof,
Ron Wuensch, Stanley Huggins (deceased),
Richard McStay, and Wally Loewenbaum.

Mentors all. Thank you!

"We find investment in private equity to be extremely concentrated. About 75% of all private equity is owned by households for whom it constitutes at least half of their total net worth. Furthermore, households with entrepreneurial equity invest on average more than 70% of their private holdings in a single private company in which they have an active management interest. Despite this dramatic lack of diversification, the average annual return to all equity in privately held companies is rather unimpressive. Private equity returns are on average no higher than the market return on all publicly traded equity."

"What we hope to convince the reader is that a complete theory of household portfolio choice should emphasize both public and private equity."

Moskovitz and Vissing Jorgensen
American Economic Review
September 2002

Table of Contents

Section I
Managing Private Company Wealth

Section 2
Tools for Managing Private Company Wealth

Section 3
Perspectives on Managing Private Company Wealth

Foreword

It's been very important to me throughout my career at Gallup that we're always better run than all of our competitors and all mid-sized consulting companies in the world. But we don't only want to be better – we also want to run our organization differently.

To do so, we've been extraordinarily intentional – relentless, in fact – about how we manage our brand, how we choose clients, the services we offer, and the people we hire. We're a bunch of do-gooders who want to change the world one client at a time. Because of that, we don't just want to sell zillions of surveys of customers, employees, and citizens around the globe – we aim to be the most helpful and influential organization in the world. And I believe we are.

We have become that organization because we've always known that to build a great company, we needed to create a workplace setting where employees could choose to be more than just paycheck-earners – that they could also own shares in this well-known privately held company. We experimented with selling employees shares in the early years, 30 to 40 years ago. But how employees got shares was unequal and the buy-sell process was messy: Some got shares as a bonus, others received what we called at the time "phantom" shares. When our Nebraska-based company, Selection Research Inc., completed its acquisition of the famous

Gallup Organization of Princeton, New Jersey, in the late 1980s, we revisited our employee stock ownership plan and decided to perfect it.

It was then that we asked Chris Mercer and his team at Mercer Capital to take us on as a client, to create a consistent, accurate, trusted system of valuing our shares quarterly and/or annually – and everything changed. We've worked closely with Chris ever since.

Chris helped us create an employee stock buy-sell program that worked. The Clifton family and employee owners purchased Gallup on October 1, 1988 and shortly following we bought and sold our first significant shares with employees at $15 per share. Twenty-five years later they were buy-selling at $800 per share. I just checked the math — this is 17.2% average compounded increase over the 25 years. Our shares are open to purchase to all employees; same price I pay, no options or special deals. As I write this, we're just finishing up buying out one of our managers who wished to sell all of his stock for $16 million. He started his career at Gallup with $0 in stock.

Our company has made many multimillionaires and we have many multimillionaires still holding and even more planting their multimillionaire seeds. At Gallup we still believe it is the American way to get as rich as you can while you are doing great things for the world. And we believe that that opportunity to get rich should be offered equally throughout the company, and especially easy for those with high wealth ambitions. Like Chris says in this book, "concentrate to create, diversify to protect." We have built a system for those who are willing to put a lot of eggs in one basket to create significant wealth.

I felt pretty good while reading the book as to how our firm stacks up on strengths and weaknesses of a privately held, internally traded company, especially when you consider the potential extreme problems that many family controlled companies can face as they go from one generation to another. Sure, we still have a lot of work to do. But because of all we have learned from Chris Mercer – all of the material now available within this book – we are doing that work very effectively and successfully, and I believe we're a great role model for all mid-sized companies in the world because we are Mercer true believers.

Not only have we seriously managed wealth creation but we've also managed wealth-sharing in a unique way. Our Vice Chairman and CFO, Jim Krieger, is probably the best sitting CFO in world on this subject for any employee-owned company. He and his teams have designed, engineered, and executed our system to perfection. Without putting words in his mouth, I believe he would say that he learned most of what he knows on the subject of valuation for buy-sell from our longtime relationship with Chris Mercer, whom we believe is the best advisor in the world on the subject.

There's one point I'd like to add to Chris' book. When a company's valuation and subsequent buy-sell program is right and perfect – when the concepts have become deeply ingrained and trusted and believed by management and employees – this not only creates wealth for individuals, it also creates a spirit that few companies possess: a spirit of "this is my company." When employees have real shares – real shares that they have purchased on their own, not given; just like the CEO bought his – they do their jobs differently because they are "all in." They are all-in because everything is suddenly fair, and achieving this is a leadership breakthrough.

If every privately held company in America suddenly subscribed to everything in this book, it would unlock a whole new spirit of ownership-based employee engagement across approximately 50 million employees--about half of all full time workers. This would boom national GDP and almighty job growth like nothing ever seen before. It would change economics and human development, and most certainly change the world.

Jim Clifton
Chairman and CEO, Gallup
Author, The Coming Jobs War

Acknowledgments

It takes a village to raise or to birth a book. This book has benefited from the help of many people.

Thanks to all those who read the book and provided the words of praise that precede this acknowledgment. You create hope that this book will really help business owners and their advisers.

Jim Clifton, Chairman and CEO of Gallup, wrote the foreword to the book. In the Foreword, he challenges us all to spread the message of the need to manage illiquid wealth to all business owners and advisers. Thank you, Jim, for your kind words about the book and about me. Without the many experiences of working with long-time clients like you and Gallup, this book would not exist.

Special thanks to Peter Stark, a friend from the National Speakers Association, for brainstorming with me, Bill Bachrach and others about the book. And thank you for your efforts working with the content and providing the title for the book!

Another thanks to Ian Campbell, author of *50 Hurdles: Business Transition Simplified*. He read an early draft of the book and his thoughtful comments contributed to the elimination of inconsistencies and to the addition of an important new chapter.

My friends and colleagues at Mercer Capital have helped in so many ways. I won't name them all here, but Matt Crow has offered continuing encouragement and help. Barbara Walters Price has been instrumental in completing this book, as well as every other book I've written. Stephanie McFall, while new to us, jumped in with the design and look of the book. I can't imagine trying to write a book without the help and support of all my friends at Mercer Capital.

Denis Boyles gave the book an editor's overview and provided numerous ideas that helped the readability of the book. Thanks, Denis.

My clients over the years, many of whom have become friends, have allowed me the privilege of working in a never-ending laboratory of learning. Every company has evolving needs for transitions of both management and ownership. I thank my clients namelessly for allowing me the privilege of talking to them about these issues and of working with a growing number of them in transition efforts.

Finally, where I have failed to listen to the good advice provided to me by so many, any remaining errors, misspellings, misstatements, or other gotchas are mine and mine alone.

October 2014
Memphis, Tennessee

Introduction

Closely held business ownership often reflects substantial concentrations of wealth. Most owners of successful closely held and family businesses have a preponderance of their personal wealth tied up in their businesses. You may have heard the term:

Concentrate to create; diversify to protect.

However, many business owners never get around to diversifying or even beginning a process of diversifying their wealth away from their businesses. Why? The most likely reason is:

Successful business owners are single-minded and their focus is on working on their companies. They believe that by managing their companies, they are managing their personal wealth.

However, that's not the case, as we will see. In addition, addressing wealth management and personal estate tax planning is often a seemingly daunting task. When you are busy and successful, you think you don't need to spend a great deal of time thinking about your future need for liquidity. That is something too often put off until tomorrow.

But you can't wait if you want to achieve reasonable results with the most important asset on your personal balance sheet.

There is a second belief held by many business owners, who tend to think that business ownership is very binary in nature. The belief might be expressed like:

Either I own the business or I don't and there's no in between. I'll just keep things as they are until I sell the business or die.

This is a self-limiting belief. It leads to doing nothing, or almost nothing, in the long interim between your current status quo and the ultimate sale or disposition of your business. You will leave your business, either horizontally or vertically. The results you achieve for yourself, your family and your fellow owners will depend in large measure on what you do between these two bookends, your current status quo and the ultimate sale or disposition of your business.

Let me say at the outset that when I speak of an ultimate sale or other disposition of your business, I'm not advocating a third party sale or any other ownership transfer strategy. However, you will transfer ownership, either in a sale, a series of partial sales, or through a series of gifts or other estate planning transactions, or through the operation of your will if you do not accomplish some or all of these activities. When I refer to an ultimate sale of your business, it is in the context of this paragraph.

About This Book

This book is written to help you understand the importance of your illiquid wealth – or the wealth locked in your private company – and present alternatives for helping you manage and eventually realize that wealth. The book has three sections.

Section I: Managing Private Company Wealth. Section I provides an overview of managing your illiquid private company wealth. In this section we introduce the wealth management concepts of diversification and asset allocation and then compare the management of liquid wealth with that of illiquid, private company wealth.

Section I also addresses the magnitude of private business wealth in America and the rationale for business owners to concentrate on diversification and on satisfactory returns from their businesses. There is a chapter discussing the rate of return on your private company investment that I hope will change how you think about your company's performance.

The final chapter in Section I introduces *The One Percent Solution*, the gist of which is simple:

> *Consider an annual budget for managing your illiquid private company wealth (defined as your ownership interest in your company) similar to the fees paid to manage your liquid wealth (stocks, bonds or other liquid assets). It costs money to manage wealth, whether liquid or illiquid so create a budget for managing your illiquid private company wealth.*

The focus of this book is on managing the wealth locked in your private business. It is not about personal estate planning, although that is certainly necessary. If you buy into *The One Percent Solution* at all, you will also engage in many of these activities as part of your overall wealth management strategy.

Section II: Tools for Managing Private Company Wealth. This section discusses many of the tools that business owners can use to manage illiquid private company wealth to achieve satisfactory shareholder returns during the interim between the current status quo and any ultimate disposition. A subtitle for Section II might be "Making the Corporate Finance Tools of the Public Markets and the Private Equity Industry Accessible to Private Businesses."

These tools include:

- **Ordinary dividend policy.** You have a dividend policy, so learn how to use it to advantage.

- **Leveraged dividends.** Obtain current liquidity and higher returns for all shareholders without selling your business.

- **Leveraged stock repurchases.** Provide liquidity for selected owners while enhancing returns for the remaining owners.

You will definitely want to discuss the ideas, tools and strategies presented in Section II with your fellow owners and your advisers.

Section III: Perspectives on Managing Private Company Wealth. This section provides several short chapters to help you understand value and to encourage thinking about your business as an investment. We discuss a number of things for you to talk about and to work on during the interim between now and any ultimate disposition, including:

- **Why businesses change hands.** You will be surprised. Unexpected things happen that mess up even well-laid plans.

- **How the *next investors* will look at your business.** If you know how future investors will look at your business, it may change the way your owners, as the current investors, begin to look at it.

- **Bad things happen to good companies.** Forewarned is forearmed. Take steps today to avoid known possible problems.

- **Is your business ready for sale?** This is a critical question whether you are ready to sell your business or not.

- **And more...**

Conclusion

This book will change the way you think about your ownership interest in your closely held or family business. Read on. Share it with your fellow owners. Share with your senior management and your key advisers. Initiate the conversations necessary to introduce or enhance the wealth management aspects of your business and personal lives.

We live our business and personal lives between the bookends of the current status quo and the ultimate sale (or other disposition) of our businesses. The interim is the time we have to do the things necessary for successful ownership and management transitions of our businesses. This book is all about focusing effort, energy and resources during the interim in order to accomplish diversification and prepare for the ultimate transitioning of both management and ownership for your company.

Think about the dash between the years of birth and death on a gravestone. Every life has a birth date and a date of death. The dates tell us when a person lived. But everything about your life and mine occurs in the dash. The bookends are always there. What matters is what we do in the interim.

Prologue

Norm and his company had been a client for a number of years. In the early years I had managed the relationship, but at the time of this story, a young analyst, Nick, was in charge.

Nick came into my office and sat down after visiting with Norm a few years ago. He told me that during the interview, Norm had complained he had just bought a $25,000 bass boat, and he had had to take out a loan to pay for it.

My immediate reaction was, "That's ridiculous!" You see, Norm's company was worth about $25 million. At the time, Norm was paid a healthy salary from the company, but the company just always seemed to absorb all of its cash flow.

The point is that Norm had virtually no liquid assets outside the company. He was embarrassed to tell about borrowing to buy the bass boat.

Further, Nick said that Norm had mentioned his wife was concerned with the couple's lack of diversification and more concerned that if something happened to Norm, she would be completely dependent on the company and their two young and untested sons for her complete support.

Nick ended his report by telling me that Norm wanted to talk to me about his situation...

SECTION I

Managing Private
Company Wealth

CHAPTER 1

Private Company Wealth Overview

Owners of successful closely held and family businesses need to focus attention on the management of *all of their wealth.* For most owners, wealth comes from two primary sources:

1. **The value of your interests in closely held or family enterprises.** This wealth is, by definition, illiquid, for there are no well-organized markets for the sale of interests in private businesses. Quite often, there is a concentration, even an extreme concentration, of wealth in this illiquid form. While businesses in their entirety can be sold, the decision to sell is often difficult, and is postponed or ignored or not agreed to by their various owners. Let's call this type of wealth *illiquid wealth.* We can also use the term *pre-liquid wealth* to signify that private wealth may be in the process, even a very long process, of becoming liquid.

2. **The value of your interests in any assets inherited, earned, derived from distributions or other transactions with your businesses, or otherwise obtained and held outside your businesses.** While such other assets might include real estate and other forms of potentially earning or appreciating assets, many owners attempt to diversify and to develop portfolios of

liquid assets outside their businesses. They do this directly and/or in retirement plans. We can call this type of wealth *liquid wealth*.

The management of *liquid wealth* is a well-organized industry in the United States. It involves legions of financial planners, tax advisers, asset management consultants and asset management firms. Liquid wealth in the United States totals many trillions of dollars and it must be managed, in many cases for fiduciary reasons.

The management of the *illiquid wealth* represented by investments in successful closely held and family businesses, on the other hand, is at best a cottage industry. As a shareholder of one or more successful private business enterprises, that wealth should be managed with the same intensity, care, concern and respect as your liquid wealth. However, many owners of successful businesses manage the wealth represented by their investments mostly by chance. There are a number of not-so-good reasons for this:

- The belief that managing the business is managing the wealth.

- It takes time and business owners don't want to do it, or else believe they cannot take the time to do it.

- It is uncomfortable talking to other owners (or a spouse or other family members) about wealth management.

- Many owners are hesitant to invest to retain competent corporate, tax, accounting, valuation and financial planning advice, or to retain (and pay for) a "quarterback," or a professional who will facilitate the investment management process.

- It is too easy to procrastinate over the always looming yet never realized plan to work on important management and ownership transition issues.

These "reasons" are really excuses and there is no excuse for not managing your wealth in a reasonable and orderly manner. It is a matter of personal and family responsibility.

Management of Illiquid Wealth Occurs During the Interim

Many business owners labor in the status quo – doing things the way they have always done them while not doing many of the things that they may know need to be done. This is natural due to daily pressures and deadlines.

Then one day something happens and there is a need or a requirement to sell the business. Chances are, neither the business nor its owner(s) are ready for a sale (see Chapter 15: "10 Reasons That Businesses Change Hands"). The overall results of this eventual sale are less favorable than they should be, either in terms of business value or shareholder readiness or both.

There are other things associated with managing the wealth you create in your business that must be accomplished in the interim between now and any ultimate disposition of your interests.

It is a given that you will spend time working in your business. However, there are other things associated with managing the wealth you create in your business that must be accomplished in the interim between now and any ultimate disposition of your interests.

For the benefit of the business and the shareholders, think about:

- Achieving and maintaining good returns for shareholders over time.

- Maintaining an optimal capital structure to facilitate shareholder returns.

- Paying appropriate dividends or distributions when satisfactory reinvestment opportunities are not present.

- Preparing and maintaining a buy-sell agreement that will work reasonably when it is triggered.

- Repurchasing shares from departing employees or other owners at appropriate times.

- Considering opportunities for returns of capital in the form of leveraged dividends or leveraged share buy-backs to accelerate shareholder returns and create opportunities for liquidity and diversification of wealth.

- Preparing for management transition at key levels in the business.

- Monitoring shareholder returns relative to comparable investment return benchmarks.

For the benefit of the shareholder(s), think about:

- Preparing and maintaining personal wills consistent with current desires for the future.

- Engaging in personal estate planning in the form of getting ownership of the business where the owners really would like it to be in the event of an unexpected sale or untimely death.

- Effecting ownership transition, either to family members through planned gifts, or to key employees through management buy-ins, employee stock ownership plans, or to outsiders.

- Planning for and achieving liquidity apart from investments in the business.

All of the above activities for businesses and shareholders relate to the management of illiquid, private company wealth.

Keep this brief overview of private company wealth management in mind as we progress through the book. There are many tools available to help manage illiquid wealth and to provide opportunities for diversification. These basic tools of corporate finance are available to you for use in your closely held or family business.

CHAPTER 2

Liquid Wealth Management

We continue our investigation of the management of *illiquid wealth* in closely held and family businesses with a discussion of *liquid wealth.* By comparing and contrasting these two general forms of wealth, we can begin to understand the principles necessary to manage illiquid wealth.

Liquid Wealth Defined

Liquid wealth is, well, liquid. Liquid wealth is comprised of securities of many kinds that are traded in active, or relatively active, markets. The wealth management business, which focuses primarily on the management of liquid wealth, is well developed. The management of illiquid wealth in closely held and family businesses is a new and developing frontier.

The market capitalization of the S&P 500 Index was some $18.5 trillion as of August 2014. There are thousands of other publicly traded companies with equity and debt securities. The bond markets include taxable and nontaxable (municipalities and states) sectors, and securitized assets of many classes now trade publicly. There is a massive amount of liquid wealth in America.

How Liquid Wealth Is Managed

Liquid wealth is typically managed by asset management firms. The top 20 such firms in the world as of June 30, 2012 (www.relbanks.com) were collectively managing almost $30 trillion *of* assets. Some of these assets are in alternative investment classes, but the majority of these funds are liquid in nature. The firms include names like Black-Rock, Inc., Vanguard, Fidelity Investments, PIMCO, and J.P. Morgan Asset Management.

In addition to these and many more titans, there are several thousand other asset management firms in the United States that have assets under management (AUM) ranging from less than $50 million upwards to many billions of dollars.

Whether your liquid funds are managed by one of the giants, or by a small, boutique, specialty firm, the customers of asset managers range from individuals to corporations to financial institutions to profit sharing and other retirement plans to insurance companies to the endowments of universities and hospitals and so on. Many owners of closely held and family businesses have liquid assets managed directly or through retirement plans with asset management firms, as well as mutual funds and other funds that may be similarly managed.

Compensation for Management of Liquid Wealth

It is almost axiomatic in the field of wealth management that money managers are compensated based on annualized percentages of the assets they have under management. The percentages might range from 20-30 basis points for bonds and other fixed income securities to 50 to 100 basis points for basic equity portfolios, to 150 basis points (1.5%) or more for private equity portfolios, venture capital funds, or hedge funds. This is not at all a criticism of asset managers. You charge for your products and services and I charge for mine. They do, too.

The point is, you and I and virtually everyone else who has liquid wealth managed by asset managers, pay regular management fees based on our AUM, or our wealth under management.

To put a number to it, assume for simplicity that an asset manager charges 1% of AUM for the management of mixed equity and fixed income portfolios. Let's introduce Mr. Jones who has a portfolio of $5 million entrusted to this manager. The manager is charging Mr. Jones at a run rate of $50 thousand per year (i.e., 1% times $5 million) for management services.

Let's hold the thought of fees for assets under management and we'll reintroduce it as we talk about private wealth in closely held and family businesses.

Diversification

The first mantra of liquid wealth management is *diversification*. According to modern portfolio theory, there are two kinds of risks that investors face with respect to securities:

- **The risk associated with individual securities.** Bad things can happen to all businesses, even good companies, and good things can happen to bad or good companies. When you own an individual security, you hope it will go up in price and it might. But disaster could strike.

- **The risks associated with the market in general.** If the market tanks, even a strongly performing company's shares may decline. Just as a rising tide lifts all boats, a falling tide takes them down.

The first solution to this mixture of risks is diversification. Modern portfolio theory suggests that if an investor owns perhaps 15-20 equity securities, the bad things that happen to some companies will, on average, be offset by good things that happen to others in an equity portfolio. The result is that a diversified portfolio of large capitalization stocks should hope to achieve the "return of the market." That is why diversification is a mantra in the management of liquid wealth. But the return of the market may be horrific for certain periods.

In business valuation, we are always concerned about concentrations, e.g., of customers. An extreme customer concentration creates risks.

> *Every customer relationship has a beginning, a duration, and an end. If the customer relationship that ends this period is your largest customer accounting for a highly disproportionate share of your sales, then bad things will happen, possibly even going out of business.*

The principal of diversification of investments is similar. You don't want to be around when one of only three or four companies in your undiversified portfolio falls on bad times and its stock price plunges, just like you don't want to be around when a single, large customer in a private business is lost.

The principal of diversification is all about managing and controlling risks associated with investment concentrations of individual securities.

Asset Allocation

Diversification is good. However, it will not protect against broad declines in the equity markets. Too recently, we all experienced the 50% drop in both the Dow Jones Industrial Index and the S&P 500 Index between October 2007 and March 2009. Basically, if you owned stocks during that period of time, your portfolio values declined.

Therefore, the second mantra of asset management is *asset allocation*. Asset allocation is a form of diversification of the mix of the various asset classes held in portfolios. Take a simple example. Assume a portfolio is invested in two diversified sub-portfolios, with one holding a mix of equity securities and the other a mix of exposure to the fixed income markets (i.e., bonds for short). Let's say that the mix is 60% equities and 40% bonds.

The theory is that the movement of stocks and bonds might be uncorrelated. This might mean that when equities are falling, general conditions in the bond market might be such that bonds hold their value or even rise in value. Or, the example could work the other way, as well. By investing in more than one asset class, the overall risk of the total portfolio should be reduced because different assets perform differently as economic and market conditions vary.

Asset allocation is really an investment strategy that seeks to balance the risks and rewards of an investment portfolio by making asset allocation decisions between asset classes based on the risk tolerances, investment time horizons and investment objectives of particular investors.

Assets might be allocated, for example to large capitalization stocks, international equities, fixed income securities, small capitalization stocks, corporate bonds, mortgage-related securities, and so on. In addition, assets are also sometimes allocated into alternative investment categories of less liquid assets, including private equity, hedge funds and a variety of other relatively illiquid categories.

Diversification Illustrated

Investors make portfolio (i.e., asset allocation) choices. Wealth managers assist them in making those choices and then, in implementing specific investment strategies designed to achieve their objectives. Recall Mr. Jones, who has $5 million of liquid assets. His financial advisor has implemented an asset allocation strategy for Mr. Jones based on the principles of diversification and asset allocation just as we have discussed.

Mr. Jones' portfolio has large capitalization stocks, smaller cap stocks, international equities, bonds and some cash. Roughly, this manager has concluded, after working with Mr. Jones, that a broad asset allocation of about 65% equities and 35% bonds and cash is appropriate, and the portfolio is invested as in the pie chart shown in Figure 1 below.

The portfolio is diversified through its asset allocation scheme and the individual components of the portfolio should be diversified as well.

Mr. Jones' portfolio manager is sleeping well at night because he has invested the portfolio in a manner that is consistent with Mr. Jones' stated objectives. This portfolio provides both income and growth prospects and the protection of the asset allocation scheme.

But read on as our story progresses. We'll learn more about Mr. Jones shortly and find out if he should be sleeping well at night.

As we pursue our discussion of illiquid wealth management, let's ask a few questions about the process of liquid wealth management.

Mr. Jones' $5 Million Portfolio

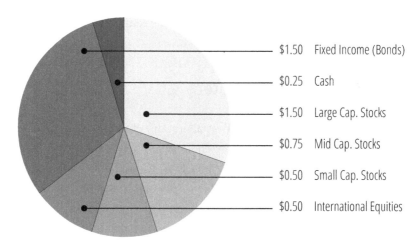

$1.50	Fixed Income (Bonds)
$0.25	Cash
$1.50	Large Cap. Stocks
$0.75	Mid Cap. Stocks
$0.50	Small Cap. Stocks
$0.50	International Equities

Figure 1

A Few Questions

What do the very wealthy in America do to manage their wealth?

The very wealthy quite often establish "family offices" through which investments are handled and a variety of personal or family planning activities are administered. By and large, these family offices hire staffs responsible for allocating assets among a variety of investment funds and strategies, seeking diversification, satisfactory (or superior) returns, and reduction in volatility, or risk. They also monitor investment performance in order to be able to recommend shifts in strategies or allocations over time. Family offices also provide tax services, record-keeping and many other services to support family members.

My "family office" is my desk at home, so I try to relate.

Let's focus on investing. The very wealthy, through their family offices, place their assets across a variety of investment classes ranging from Treasuries, to fixed income securities, to market portfolios bearing numerous names representing their "strategies," to private equity funds, and even to hedge funds. Then, there are investments in land, timber and developed real estate, either through REITs or more directly, through proprietary funds, and even direct investments.

In addition, the very wealthy are continually investigating tax-efficient ways in which to preserve their wealth and to pass it to subsequent generations, or, increasingly, to give it away (like Bill and Melinda Gates, Mark and Priscilla Chan Zuckerberg, Warren Buffet, and many others).

What do the merely wealthy in America do with their money?

In many respects, the merely wealthy do the same thing as the very wealthy, except they may outsource investment decisions to a trust department of a bank or to a variety of "multi-family offices" or investment managers.

Quite often, the merely wealthy will spend considerable time and money seeking tax and legal advice to accomplish their objectives of intergenerational wealth transfers as well as their charitable objectives.

What do the affluent in America do with their money?

Most affluent Americans place all, or at least large portions of their liquid assets, into a variety of mutual funds, or place their assets with other investment intermediaries who, in turn, place collective assets into some of the same funds used by the very wealthy or make direct investments on their behalf.

There are some who attempt to manage their money on their own. That's good for people with training or experience and the discipline to actively manage. However, many business owners lack the time or the interest to manage their liquid wealth personally.

What do the rest of Americans do with their money?

Many Americans who may have virtually no liquid assets nevertheless have assets invested on their behalf through their retirement plans at work.

The fiduciaries of these plans that deal with growing pools of assets over time are charged with the duty to invest retirement funds.

Common Themes of Liquid Wealth Management

What do the management practices for liquid wealth by the very wealthy, the merely wealthy, the affluent, and the rest of us in America have in common? There are at least two threads tying liquid wealth management together.

1. **Investment Treatment.** The first common denominator of the investing habits of most Americans is that our accumulated

liquid assets are treated like investments. They are placed in the custody of capable investment managers who handle the direct investment activities and periodic changes to our portfolios. In many instances, the managers will advise their clients regarding asset allocation and portfolio strategy and provide regular monitoring services.

2. **Management Fees.** The payment of management fees to asset or wealth managers is the second common denominator. These fees are frequently based on a percentage of assets under management and are typically paid quarterly. Returns are provided net of these asset management fees, so many people never even think about them, even though they should.

Earlier, we talked about the principles of diversification and asset allocation. It is now time to think about how those principles are employed by wealth managers.

Liquid Wealth Management Process

The wealth management process is discussed on the websites of investment firms, financial planners, money managers, insurance professionals and others. All of the descriptions of the process involve common elements as shown in Figure 2.

The principal of diversification is all about managing and controlling risks associated with investment concentrations of individual securities.

The circular planning process involves least several discrete steps. While the process relates to liquid wealth management, we relate the process steps to your private business investments, as well.

1. **Set overall objectives.** A wise man once said, "If you don't know where you are going, any road will do." Managing wealth is too important not to consider in the context of circumstances in

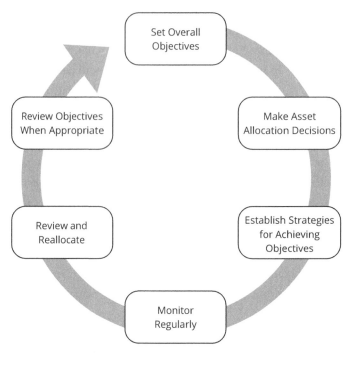

Figure 2

existence at any point in time. *You need to establish your overall investment objectives in light of your business ownership and all your other assets.*

2. **Make asset allocation decisions.** Asset allocation decisions are important. If you invest, you have to decide in what sector or sectors you will invest in and then, what specific securities you will acquire. There is an often-mentioned thought that asset allocation decisions determine some 90% of long-term returns from investing. One study actually concluded that asset allocation decisions account for 90% of the *variability of returns* across managers. We don't know what portion of investment returns asset allocation provides, but allocation decisions are clearly important, if only as a means of diversifying the risks associated

with particular markets. One quick takeaway at this point: *You should be focused on your asset allocation and risk profile, inclusive of your business ownership.*

3. **Establish strategies for achieving allocation and objectives.** Where will you invest and with whom? Will you use a single manager, multiple managers, or a fund-of-funds concept? Who will help you evaluate performance and progress toward objectives? *This principle of setting strategies is especially important when it comes to concentrated investments in relatively illiquid private businesses.*

4. **Monitor Regularly.** Many, if not most investment managers report summary performance on a monthly basis (or even daily in some cases). Virtually all managers provide detailed performance reports on a quarterly basis.

    Many people work with financial planners or other wealth managers. There tends to be a relatively high degree of ongoing communication regarding portfolio performance. Let me ask this question: *What do you do to monitor the value of your business in relation to the rest of your wealth?* If you are like many business owners, the answer is either not much or nothing at all. *You should consider obtaining an annual, or every other year at least, appraisal to monitor your business investment performance and returns.*

5. **Review and reallocate.** Performance over time will cause asset allocations to change as one sector outperforms another. It may be necessary to reallocate funds from one investment sector, say large capitalization stocks after a period of robust growth, to other sectors to maintain overall asset allocations. *Reallocation does not occur automatically or even easily in private businesses. We will discuss reallocation strategies later, but dividend policy is a good place to start.*

6. **Revise objectives, when appropriate.** As circumstances change, it may be appropriate to revise investment objectives, and so the process begins anew.

Wealth managers who work with liquid assets are intimately familiar with these steps, or investment principles, and work with their clients through an ongoing process of setting objectives, deciding on asset allocations and establishing strategies.

Recall that we live life in the interim between our current status quo and any eventual sale or disposition of our business. Implementing a wealth management process that involves all of your assets, including your business investment, is a worthwhile effort. Your ultimate success in achieving your personal wealth management goals will be determined by what you do in the interim.

CHAPTER 3

Managing Private Company Wealth Is A Big Deal

Wealth management for illiquid assets like in your closely held or family business is a big deal that is ignored by too many business owners. We use the term, "pre-liquid," to describe this wealth because that's how you think about it.

Your company is with you today. Someday, perhaps a long time from now, you are going to sell it. Right? Then, you will have liquid wealth. So, today, your wealth is pre-liquid. But there are many things you can do in the interim, between now and an eventual sale, to manage your pre-liquid wealth.

Wealth management principles are well established for liquid assets as we have seen. The picture is quite different when the typical wealth manager encounters pre-liquid assets. Wealth managers simply do not know how to address such illiquid assets. They do not fit into any of the typical investment classes.

Regardless, the management of the illiquid wealth locked into your closely held or family business is a big deal for you, your family, your fellow owners, your employees and, indeed, all of your stakeholders.

Pre-liquid assets either become liquid or facilitate the creation of liquid assets when they are sold (entire businesses or partial sales).

Pre-liquid assets generate potentially liquid assets when economic distributions (i.e., distributions net of associated taxes) are made to their owners.

Pre-Liquid Wealth Represents Real Money

We are talking about real money when we discuss pre-liquid assets. Professors Moskowitz and Vissing Jorgensen, writing in the prestigious *American Economic Review* (September, 2002), suggest that the magnitude of private equity and public equity held by households were similar in magnitude, at least through the 1990s, the period of their study. The article is titled "The Returns to Entrepreneurial Investment: A Private Equity Premium Puzzle?"

The professors found it puzzling that households routinely invest substantial amounts in a single privately held firm with a seemingly far worse risk-return trade-off than investing in liquid wealth. We will incorporate some of the professors' observations into our discussion of managing private wealth.

As of 1998, the professors estimated the value of private equity held by households in the United States was $5.7 trillion. Inflation adjusted, the number would exceed $8 trillion today. In the book, *The $10 Trillion Opportunity*, published in 2005, authors Richard Jackim and Peter Christman estimated that private businesses worth some $10 trillion would be sold in the next decade. Similar predictions continue to be made today.

We know two things. First, there is a huge amount of wealth locked into private businesses in America. We also know that the tsunami of business sales predicted by Jackim and Christman has not yet occurred. We had a financial crisis in 2007-2009 that severely reduced transactions involving private companies. We have not yet returned to pre-recession transaction volumes.

An interesting study, "Baby Boomer Business Owners: Will There Be a Mass Sell-Off?," makes important observations about the age distribution of business ownership (Carey McMann, SME Research, September 2002):

- Well more than half of all businesses in America are owned by baby boomers (currently aged 50 – 67) and the still older silent generation.

- Baby boomers are still starting businesses, with 21% of all start-ups during 2011 having owners 55-64 years of age.

- 37% of businesses have owners with ages of 55 years or older.

The study concludes that perhaps 20% to 25% of all businesses in America will be sold or otherwise change hands over the next five-to-ten years.

Any way you care to cut it, there is a large and growing number of business owners in the United States who are in their 50s, 60s, 70s, and even older, who will sell their businesses in the coming years, or die in the saddle and burden their families, who will have to deal with their messes.

A True Story and the Ownership Transfer Matrix

Henry was in his mid-80s when age caught up with him. After selling below control a few years prior in a leveraged stock redemption, Henry caused the company to continue purchasing shares from departing employees and other shareholders. As a result of these repurchases, Henry's ownership crept up above 50%.

After his death, Henry's estate was valued on a controlling interest basis, rather than on an illiquid minority basis. The good news is that his wife was somewhat younger and in good health. Hopefully some good planning will take place so that the control block, which passed to her through the estate, will be reduced to a minority interest.

The point is that Henry didn't pay attention during the interim between his leveraged stock redemption and his death and created potentially expensive problems as a result.

Most business owners think of their ownership as binary. "I own it now and someday, I won't." Henry never sold his company. And today, he doesn't own it any longer. Examine the Ownership Transfer Matrix in Figure 3. It makes this critical point:

> *There's no way outside the boxes, so it is best to plan what for happens inside them.*

The Ownership Transfer Matrix

	Partial Sale/Transfer	Total Sale/Transfer
Voluntary Transfer	ESOP Outside Investor(s) Sales to Insiders/Relatives Combination Merger/Cash Out Going Public Gifting Programs Buy-Sell Agreements	Sale of Business Stock-for-Stock Exchange with Public Company Stock Cash Sale to Public Company Installment Sale to Relatives/Insiders ESOP/Management Buyout Liquidation Buy-Sell Agreements
Involuntary Transfer	Death Divorce Forced Restructuring Shareholder Disputes Buy-Sell Agreements	Death Divorce Forced Restructuring Bankruptcy Shareholder Disputes Liquidation Buy-Sell Agreements

Figure 3

Simply put, there is a lot of wealth tied up in closely held and family businesses, and a lot of that wealth is owned by Baby Boomers and their parents. All of these business owners will engage in one or more of the transfers outlined above. You will transfer your business ownership interest. The transfers may be partial or total. And they may be voluntary or involuntary. Have any of the transfer items in the boxes above happened to you?

Private Company Wealth is Concentrated

Was the example of Mr. Jones' portfolio in the prior chapter realistic? Listen to the professors:

> *"We find investment in private equity to be extremely concentrated.* ***About 75% of all private equity is owned by households for whom it constitutes at least half of their total net worth.*** *Furthermore, households with entrepreneurial equity invest on average more than 70% of their private holdings in a single private company in which they have an active management interest. Despite this dramatic lack of diversification, the average annual return to all equity in privately held companies is rather unimpressive. Private equity returns are on average no higher than the market return on all publicly traded equity." (emphasis added)*

We will talk about the returns we realize from closely held and family businesses in the next section of the book. But think about the implications of this study.

Look at the typical wealth manager's considerations of liquid and pre-liquid assets for the same clients.

Very few wealth managers are involved in setting investment objectives *for the substantial pre-liquid assets held by some of their clients*. If they do not help set objectives, it is difficult to be involved in establishing strategies.

\any cases, the wealth manager is attempting to help his or
thout specific knowledge of what is likely the largest single
lient's portfolio.

> On a risk adjusted basis, many private companies achieve lower returns than those available in the public securities markets. Not good.

Worse still from an adviser's viewpoint, when clients obtain liquidity from their closely held and family businesses in a sale transaction, they may seek larger, better known wealth managers for this newly obtained liquidity – especially if the existing wealth managers were not involved in the owner's decision-making process beforehand.

We recently spoke to Samantha, a successful wealth planner who works primarily with private businesses in the middle market. She observed that it is extremely rare for business owners to hold meetings with their key advisers at the same time, and that virtually none of the advisors has any unified concept of what the owner's financial planning should entail.

Samantha said:

> *In fact, each of the advisers has his or her own agenda for working with business owner clients, and there is never, well, almost never, any concept of a coordinated program for the businesses, the owners' estates, or for ownership or management transition planning.*

That's what we are talking about.

Do owners of closely held and family businesses typically think about their pre-liquid assets as investments? Not if our experience is representative.

The bottom line is that liquid wealth tends to be very closely managed, while pre-liquid wealth is not usually managed very closely at all.

As a business owner, you may be thinking: "Why, of course, my pre-liquid wealth is managed. I run the business every day."

The business should be run everyday. However, that's not the point at all. In fact, the comment helps make the point.

- **Every company, public or private, is managed (to greater or lesser degree).** What we are talking about is managing the pre-liquid wealth in private companies and creating strategies for converting that wealth from pre-liquid to liquid form over time through enhanced performance, distributions, partial sales, or ultimately, the sale of the businesses.

- **The business owner who manages a business every day tends not to think longer-term about when and how the wealth in the business will be realized.** That business owner is seldom thinking about how to use the business to create liquid assets to facilitate diversification away from the primary asset, which is, of course, the business.

The professors quoted previously explain the need to manage pre-liquid assets:

> *What we hope to convince the reader is that a complete theory of household portfolio choice should emphasize both public and private equity.*

The fact is that pre-liquid wealth is often not managed at all, and is seldom managed to the degree typically found with liquid wealth.

Disparity Between Management of Pre-Liquid and Liquid Wealth

What are some of the implications of the disparity of management of pre-liquid wealth and liquid wealth?

1. **Substantial management fees paid to wealth managers for managing liquid assets.** As I am writing, I received the quarterly statement from our profit sharing and 401-k plan. A quick calculation shows that we are paying management fees of about 70 basis points for the management of those tax-deferred funds in our plans.

2. **Little use of investment principles by wealth managers as applied to pre-liquid assets.** Few businesses actually calculate a rate of return for their closely held investments each year. Many business owners have never paid a distribution.

3. **Virtually no "management fees" paid for managing pre-liquid assets.** We are not aware of any financial consultants or wealth managers who work with business owners to manage pre-liquid wealth and charge fees based on a percentage of assets under management.

4. **Inadequate attention paid to the management aspects of pre-liquid wealth.** Too few business owners have a coordinated plan to diversify their wealth over time and to plan for their need for ultimate liquidity – when they either cannot or will not want to work in the future.

5. **Inadequate attention to basic corporate finance techniques designed to enhance value.** We will talk about a number of these tools later in the book, but for now, we are focusing on things like dividend policy, balance sheet management, share repurchase plans, and recapitalizations to take funds out of the business while still maintaining ownership.

6. **Almost no attention paid by business owners to the critical monitoring and enhancing investment principles, and to the reallocation of pre-liquid wealth into liquid form.** The professors point out that returns to private company equity are not adequate, on average, from a risk-adjusted point of view. It is

easy to get comfortable with our businesses and to let important planning and investment principles wait. It is easy to let excess assets accumulate inside your business where they dampen your investment returns and mess up your balance sheet. It is easy to avoid paying dividends because you think, in your infinite wisdom, that it is inappropriate for your shareholders (your kids?) to have this source of return. What would you say if the public companies you invest in, directly or indirectly, did the same thing? It is easy to let things slide during the interim between your current status quo and your ultimate disposition of your business.

Just to be clear, let's ask this question directly:

What do many, if not most, closely held and family business owners do to manage the wealth tied up in their closely held business?

For many, the answer to the question is "not much." It is time to focus on managing your private wealth.

Liquid wealth management is serious business. Pre-liquid wealth management should receive the same degree of attention and respect as that of liquid wealth management. The costs of not doing so are simply too high. There is much to be done in the interim between your current status quo and the ultimate sale or other disposition of your business.

CHAPTER 4

The Rate of Return on Your Private Company Investment

If you have funds invested with asset managers, you almost certainly get monthly or quarterly reports on performance, typically measuring the return on your portfolio for the preceding month, quarter or year. The performance of your portfolio will be benchmarked against appropriate indices of comparable investments. Unfortunately, this concept of managing wealth by reporting on financial performance does not exist with most closely held and family companies.

You own a substantial interest in a private company. What was the return on your investment in that business last year? And how did it compare with relevant benchmarks? What are the relevant benchmarks? All important questions. Let's investigate.

What is the Return on a Portfolio?

The concept of portfolio return is fairly straightforward. What is the return, in terms of dividends and change in portfolio value, for a period (say a year), in relationship to the beginning value of the portfolio? Stated algebraically, the return on a portfolio is:

$$\text{Annual Return} = \frac{\left(\text{Dividends} + \begin{array}{c}\text{Realized} \\ \text{Capital Gains}\end{array} + \begin{array}{c}\text{Unrealized} \\ \text{Appreciation}\end{array} \right)}{\text{Beginning Value of a Portfolio}}$$

You get reports from your asset managers providing this information.

Asset Returns are Important

The reason to work *on* a business is to increase its return, or yield. In the context of an owner's overall portfolio, the reason to work on the business is to increase the total yield, or return, of the entire portfolio.

How important is this concept? Recall the pie charts showing liquid assets and total asset allocations for Mr. Jones. First let's look at his liquid portfolio in Figure 4.

Assume that his wealth manager has invested well, and that the total return, net of fees on the $5 million liquid portfolio, was 11.8% for the

Mr. Jones' $5 Million Portfolio

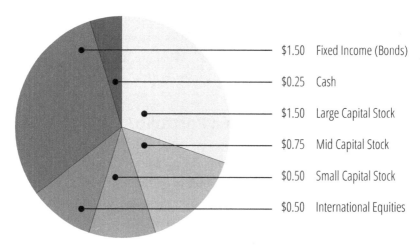

$1.50	Fixed Income (Bonds)
$0.25	Cash
$1.50	Large Capital Stock
$0.75	Mid Capital Stock
$0.50	Small Capital Stock
$0.50	International Equities

Figure 4

year just ended, based on strong equity returns and low single digit returns for bonds and cash. Assume for perspective that the broad market increased 11.0% that year. The wealth manager produced stellar returns from a diversified portfolio and beat the market with a diversified liquid portfolio that had less risk (lower volatility) than the market. Mr. Jones should be pleased.

Now, however, assume that his business is worth $20 million, raising the total portfolio value to $25 million, as seen in Figure 5.

The return from the business last year (dividends plus increase in value) was only 7.0%. However, the heavy weighting of this single asset (80% of the portfolio) and its relatively low return lowered Mr. Jones' total return to an overall 8.0%. The math is straightforward:

$$(80\% \text{ Weight x } 7\% \text{ Return}) + (20\% \text{ Weight x } 11.8\% \text{ Return})$$
$$= 8.0\% \text{ Portfolio Return}$$

Mr. Jones' $25 Million Portfolio

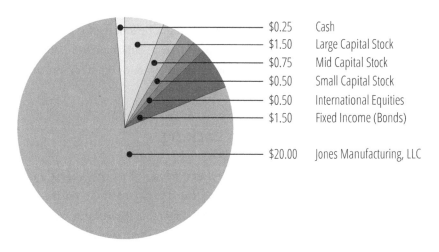

$0.25	Cash
$1.50	Large Capital Stock
$0.75	Mid Capital Stock
$0.50	Small Capital Stock
$0.50	International Equities
$1.50	Fixed Income (Bonds)
$20.00	Jones Manufacturing, LLC

Figure 5

Recall the previous discussion about returns on private wealth. Professors Moskovitz and Vissing-Jorgensen wrote the following [repeating, with my comments in brackets]:

> We find investment in private equity to be extremely concentrated. **About 75% of all private equity is owned by households for whom it constitutes at least half of their total net worth.** [This is certainly true of Mr. Jones, where private equity accounts for 80% of his household's wealth]. Furthermore, households with entrepreneurial equity invest on average more than 70% of their private holdings in a single private company in which they have an active management interest. [Also true for Mr. Jones]. **Despite this dramatic lack of diversification, the average annual return to all equity in privately held companies is rather unimpressive.** Private equity returns are on average no higher than the market return on all publicly traded equity. [And, in Mr. Jones' case, his company delivered a sub-public market return or yield, despite the fact that it is a riskier investment than a basket of publicly traded securities] (emphasis added)

If the wealth manager had produced a return of 8.0% in an 11% market for Mr. Jones' liquid portfolio, Mr. Jones might be looking for another manager. Mr. Jones and his team produced a 7.0% return for their shareholders and most likely, no one is even aware of the total return for the business.

Valuation Information Lacking

Unfortunately, many business owners never have the valuation information necessary to make the calculation of their business investment returns, and few wealth managers have the information necessary to incorporate return estimates into their overall planning for their clients.

Interested wealth managers will encourage clients with private business wealth to obtain regular valuations to make such calculations and to work on the business if returns are inadequate.

You own a substantial interest in a private company. What was the return on your investment in that business last year?

Assume that Mr. Jones received no dividends and realized no capital gains from his investment in his company during the year just ended. We assumed that his return from that investment was 7.0% during the year. To calculate this rate of return for shareholders, we need the beginning price and the ending price, which would require appraisals at the end of the prior year and at the end of the most recent year.

If the $20 million in value for the business was invested with his money manager, Mr. Jones would be paying an additional $200 thousand in wealth management fees (1.0% of $20 million). Hold that thought and see the next chapter.

The rate of return on your private company investment is an important determinate of your overall portfolio return and, ultimately, the wealth available for retirement and other personal goals. It pays to pay attention.

CHAPTER 5

The One Percent Solution

To understand *The One Percent Solution,* we first need to understand what it is not. This concept has little at all to do with managing your business. Businesses create wealth. Business schools talk about management and supply chains and marketing and many other aspects of businesses. Business schools, however, do very little to teach how to manage the wealth created by closely held and private businesses.

So how can business owners begin to better manage the wealth in their businesses? We now examine *The One Percent Solution.*

The One Percent Solution

What is the solution to financing the expenditures necessary to manage the wealth tied up in closely held and family businesses? The solution is so obvious that we overlook it, thinking that such activities either are too expensive, too time-consuming, or worse, not a high priority.

For business owners, the solution lies in the decision to treat their ownership interests as investments. The process begins with *The One Percent Solution.*

Consider an annual budget for managing your illiquid private company wealth (defined as your ownership interest in your company) similar to fees paid to manage your liquid wealth (stocks, bonds or other liquid assets). It costs money to manage wealth, whether liquid or illiquid, so create a budget for managing your illiquid private company wealth.

The One Percent Solution suggests allocating a *percentage of value* for the illiquid assets *under management* to provide the budget necessary to manage wealth. There is no formula for the precise percentage of conceptual value for the management fee. We are promoting the concept and not any particular percentage.

If the wealth were liquid, that budget would be 1% of assets under management, plus or minus, depending on the asset categories of investment. For pre-liquid wealth, we suggest considering a budget for investment management on the order of 100 basis points (1%) or so of value. If, after planning is instituted, the budget can be lowered on an ongoing basis, fine. If you want to start smaller, do so. The important thing is to start. Momentum builds with motion and momentum is key to long-term achievement of personal wealth management goals.

Your budget would also likely scale down as a percentage of value (AUM) as value increases. There is only so much "management" that will make sense at any point in time.

Figure 6 illustrates the concept of *The One Percent Solution* for companies of varying sizes and values. The "management fee" as a percentage of value scales down as the value increases, as does the relative size of the fee in relationship to earnings.

The last column in Figure 6 calculates the "management fee" as a percentage of assumed pre-tax earnings. This is to highlight that management activities are not free and that there are real expenses associated with managing pre-liquid wealth.

The One Percent Solution For Managing Pre-Liquid Wealth

Assumed Pre-Tax Income ($000)	Assumed Valuation Multiple	Estimated Value of Business Equity ($000)	Management Fee as % of Value	One Percent Management Fee Budget ($000)	Management Fee as % of Earnings
$1,250	4.00	$5,000	1.00%	$50	4.0%
$2,500	4.50	$11,250	1.00%	$113	4.5%
$5,000	5.00	$25,000	1.00%	$250	5.0%
$10,000	6.00	$60,000	0.50%	$300	3.0%
$20,000	7.00	$140,000	0.40%	$560	2.8%
$50,000	8.00	$400,000	0.25%	$1,000	2.0%
$100,000	10.00	$1,000,000	0.10%	$1,000	1.0%

Figure 6

Focus on the middle row in the figure where pre-tax income is $10.0 million. If the appropriate valuation multiple is 6x, the business is worth $60 million. We assumed that the appropriate management fee is 50 basis points of this value, or $300 thousand. That turns out to be 3.0% of reported earnings. The figure shows illustrative examples for both higher- and lower-earnings companies.

If you are a business owner, you may be thinking: "That budget is just too much!" Don't fall into that negative trap before reading on. The budget range above is for illustrative purposes only. So don't think negatively before understanding the benefits to you, your family and your fellow owners of engaging in a serious wealth management process for your pre-liquid wealth.

Let's look at how this *One Percent Solution* budget might be employed and obtain a glimpse of what it might accomplish in the wealth management process.

One Percent Solution Activities

What would your *One Percent Solution* budget be spent on? There are a number of possibilities:

1. **Wealth Manager Compensation.** The wealth manager who introduces *One Percent Solution* concepts to business owners may seek compensation based on a percentage of the value of the business, or based on specific fees. Wealth managers for private businesses include financial planners, attorneys, accountants, valuation professionals, and other consultants who work with business owners to help manage their wealth. You will pay some of these professionals at their regular hourly billing rates, but that's all part of your *One Percent Solution* budget for managing your pre-liquid wealth. You pay similar fees for management of your liquid wealth and probably never think about it. It is time to think about your illiquid wealth and its management.

2. **Annual Appraisals and Monitoring of Performance.** Liquid assets are valued every day, and portfolio performance reports are made at least quarterly for most portfolios. Annual valuation of closely held companies is the best way of tracking investment performance over time, and for reporting to shareholders about a company's return performance relative to itself and to other asset categories.

   We have been advocating the benefits of annual, or at least periodic, appraisal of businesses for many years. When I speak to business owners I sometimes joke and say that in the early years, I encouraged annual appraisals because they would be good for my business! Now, after many years of working with private businesses, I unabashedly make the recommendation because *it is good business.* My firm, Mercer Capital, provides annual appraisals for more than 100 companies. Some of these companies have been clients for 25 or more years. Mercer Capital also obtains an independent appraisal each year for the purposes of our ESOP. We use the appraisal for other planning purposes, as well (including our buy-sell agreement). There is clearly value in the process.

Recall that Mr. Jones might set a $200 thousand *One Percent Solution* budget for managing the $20 million of wealth in his business. The appraisals necessary to monitor shareholder returns would cost a fraction of this annual budget.

3.   **Buy-Sell Agreement Pricing.** Annual valuations can also establish the value for buy-sell agreements. They are so important that I have written a print book (*Buy-Sell Agreements for Closely Held and Family Business Owners*) and an Amazon Kindle book (*Buy-Sell Agreements for Baby Boomer Business Owners*) about these critical and oft-ignored business agreements. In fact, the valuation process I most often recommend is that a single appraiser be agreed upon by the parties and employed to provide an initial valuation for buy-sell agreements, and then that the appraiser will provide annual revaluations to update the price for the buy-sell agreement. Note that the annual appraisal for purposes of your buy-sell agreement would serve multiple purposes. (See www.mercercapital.com or www.ChrisMercer. net/books.)

4.   **Life Insurance Funding.** *The One Percent Solution* budget could certainly include the cost of life insurance purchased on the lives of key shareholders to fund stock purchases from deceased owners in accordance with buy-sell agreement provisions. The annual valuation can establish the amount of life insurance needed, and be a prompt for necessary adjustments to the amounts purchased as value changes over time.

Let me make the following point about life insurance and buy-sell agreements. It is essential that the owners agree, in advance, about how life insurance proceeds will be treated for valuation purposes. It is also essential that the language in the buy-sell agreement and any related documents be consistent and crystal clear. The life insurance issue is treated in some detail both in the print book and the Amazon Kindle book mentioned above. (See www.mercercapital.com or www.ChrisMercer.net/books.)

5. **Estate Planning.** Tax counsel could be retained to provide ongoing advice regarding gift and estate planning issues for shareholders. Good estate planning takes time. You may need to work with family or personal consultants as well to help work through family issues like which children get the stock of the business and how much, and which children get other assets. Are there enough other assets for a "fair" (you define) resolution?

6. **Ownership Transition Planning.** Not all closely held businesses are family businesses. It is often necessary to consider the orderly transitioning of ownership to others if a business owner is going to be able to engage in a reasonable exit at some point. Ownership transition is all about having value where it needs to be when it needs to be there. More than a few business owners have made undocumented promises to share ownership with key employees. If those promises have been made, they need to be delivered. Failure to do so will create problems later, perhaps major problems, if and when the company is sold.

7. **Financial Planning.** Key owners and shareholders could retain personal financial advisers to assist with their personal financial planning. The annual valuation will assist financial planners in advising with respect to asset allocation decisions for non-business assets.

8. **Annual Legal Review.** It is helpful to have legal counsel review a company's board of directors' minutes and other legal docu-

ments and contracts on a periodic basis. This practice helps to identify and eliminate issues that, left alone, can create potential problems in the future. The investment management budget would also include an annual review of the buy-sell agreement by legal counsel and business advisers. Numerous other corporate documents require annual or periodic review, including insurance documents and insurance coverages.

9. **Outside Board Members.** It may be appropriate to retain one or more qualified outside board members. Their independent guidance and experience can be extremely useful in maintaining the integrity of investment performance. They should also bring the benefit of diversified experience to your business.

10. **Corporate Finance for Private Businesses.** It can also cost money to have qualified financial advisors explore corporate finance solutions for your private business. Your business may be a candidate to engage in a leveraged share repurchase, or a special dividend, or a leveraged dividend recapitalization, or any of several other potential avenues to create partial liquidity and diversification for its owners – without selling the business.

So you see, there are many things that you can do to begin to focus on managing the pre-liquid wealth in your business. But know that all of these activities occur in the interim between your current status quo and the ultimate sale or disposition of your business.

A "Free" Million Dollars

Any dollar spent is certainly not available for distribution or reinvestment, so investment management expenses are definitely not free. However, *One Percent Solution* expenses become almost free when returns are enhanced to more than offset the expenses, and when dollars spent on annual valuations, life insurance policies, estate planning, financial

The One Percent Solution suggests allocating a percentage of value for the illiquid assets under management to provide the budget necessary to manage wealth.

planning, etc., are added back to earnings by buyers in the their processes of "normalizing" earnings.

In other words, while dollars spent on investment management activities do reflect real expenses, the returns on their investments may exceed the actual investments and may be capitalizable at the time of any ultimate sale of a business.

This point is easy to misunderstand, so let's look at the case of Mr. Jones and his company. If Mr. Jones had already adopted *The One Percent Solution,* his annual budget for wealth management would be $200 thousand at a 1.0% AUM fee rate. The company has $4 million in reported pre-tax income, which, in our hypothetical valuation was valued at a multiple of 5x, yielding the assumed $20 million in value.

"Non-normal" operating expenses associated with ownership and management transitions as outlined above are often "normalized" and added to pro forma earnings by many buyers. At the present time, this may be possible, because most companies do not spend any or much money on managing owners' wealth, so these expenses may well be considered to be normalizing adjustments by potential buyers.

Assume now we can document $200 thousand in *One Percent Solution* activities for Mr. Jones' company. Normalized earnings are therefore $4.2 million and the business is worth $21.0 million rather than $20.0 million. Not much, but after all, what's a "free" $1 million among friends? Would you rather have it or not? Almost a free lunch? Maybe.

Conclusion

The One Percent Solution is an important concept for owners of closely held and family businesses. You want to manage your business, of course. But you also need to manage the wealth that your business creates for you and your family and your fellow owners.

If all of this seems overwhelming, start small. Begin with a review of your buy-sell agreement with legal counsel, a competent valuation adviser, your personal and corporate financial advisers, and your life insurance adviser(s). You have to start somewhere.

Consider allocating a percentage, say 50 basis points (0.5%) or 100 basis points (1.0%) as the initial budget, for beginning to manage your pre-liquid wealth. The return on your investment will undoubtedly be substantial. Your shareholders may enjoy more liquidity and diversification. You and your family will have peace of mind.

CHAPTER 6

Valuation Concepts for Ownership and Management Transition

To complete Section I of this book, which introduces the topic of managing private company wealth, we introduce valuation concepts that are important for the ongoing discussion.

Business owners are sometimes confused about the value of their businesses – and rightly so. Simply put, there is no such thing as "the value" of a business at a point in time. Business value is a range concept with value being a function of the specific interest, time and purpose. Specifically, consider the following "values" for one business at single point in time.

- The fair market value of the common stock (100%) of the business for purposes of its buy-sell agreement, which calls for an appraisal at the financial control level of value, is $100 per share.

- The investment value of the same business to its most likely strategic acquirer is $130 per share based on the potential acquirer's analysis of potential synergies in combination with its own operations.

- The fair market value of a 5% interest in the business for gift tax purposes is determined by appraisal to be $65 per share based on consideration of the investment characteristics of the 5% minority interest. The appraiser valued the business at the marketable minority level of value at $100 per share and determined that a 35% marketability discount was appropriate, resulting in the discounted value of $65 per share.

These concepts are familiar to many business owners and their advisers; however, differing values for different purposes does create confusion and misunderstanding about the nature of business value and valuation. Each separate value was determined from the viewpoint of relevant investors for the interest being valued based on the investment characteristics of each interest.

Appraisers use a chart like Figure 7 to describe the various "levels" of value.

The Levels of Value

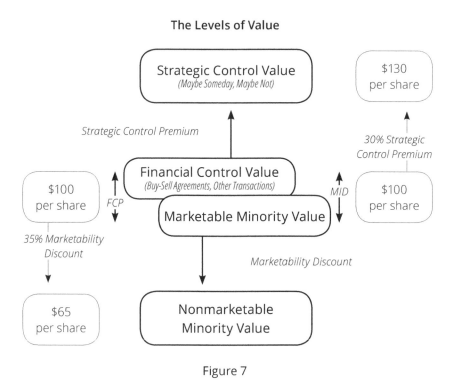

Figure 7

Figure 7 illustrates the conceptual levels of value and emphasizes the fact that value exists along a continuum based on the size of the interest in a company being valued, for example, 10% or 100% of the stock) and the purpose under consideration. The three different values noted above are shown in the chart, and "the value" of this business ranges from $65 per share to $130 per share depending on the purpose in question and the viewpoints of buyers and sellers.

To further complicate the issue of business value from the viewpoint of business owners, it really doesn't matter what you think the value of your company or your stock is or should be. The only thing that matters in the interim between now and any ultimate sale or disposition of your business is what I (or another) qualified appraiser thinks based on an appraisal process. At the time of any ultimate sale, the only thing that matters is the value conclusion of the highest bidder for your company, and whether that bidder is a strategic buyer or a financial buyer.

An understanding of the levels of value and their differences is important when discussing management and ownership transitions. Before looking at the levels, let's introduce another term, the standard of value known as *fair market value.*

Fair market value is a hypothetical standard that developed primarily in the context of the gift and estate tax world. The term was defined and elaborated upon by the Internal Revenue Service in its Revenue Ruling 59-60, published in 1959, which defines fair market value as, in effect:

> *The price at which the property would change hands between a willing buyer and a willing seller when the former is not under any compulsion to buy and the latter is not under any compulsion to sell, both parties having reasonable knowledge of relevant facts. Court decisions frequently state in addition that the hypothetical buyer and seller are assumed to be able, as well as willing, to trade and to be well informed about the property and concerning the market for such property.*

> At the time of any ultimate sale, the only thing that matters is the value conclusion of the highest bidder for your company, and whether that bidder is a strategic buyer or a financial buyer.

Fair market value is a hypothetical concept. Appraisers use this standard to mirror the thinking of hypothetical investors in reaching hypothetical prices at which hypothetical transactions take place. Business owners, however, live in the real world and engage in real transactions involving real people and real assets.

The concept of fair market value and the related levels of value that have been developed in the context of fair market value determinations is important because it provides guidance for and pricing for many actual transactions in real life. So we will look at the levels of value briefly.

Strategic Control Level

The strategic control level of value is the topmost level in the conceptual levels of value chart in Figure 7.

The strategic control level of value represents value from the viewpoint of potential strategic, or synergistic, buyers for a company. Fair market value is a hypothetical concept and is usually considered to be one of financial control for controlling interests, unless the typical buyers for a business are strategic in nature.

Relatively few appraisals are rendered at the strategic control level of value. This level of value is normally observed in the marketplace when whole companies are sold. They are sold based on negotiations between real parties who bring their relative strengths, biases and motivations to the market. Transactional values are also influenced by the relative attractiveness of a company and by the level of competition for the asset.

Vague notions of their strategic control values often hamper business owners when thinking about either management or ownership transitions. It is too easy for binary thinking to enter the picture. "Either I own the business or I don't, and when I sell, I'll sell for a strategic price."

This binary notion is really not a good way of thinking about business ownership for at least two reasons:

- **Not every business will not attract strategic buyers or receive that level of pricing in a transaction.** Many, if not most transactions occur at what we can call a financial control level of pricing. Either the buyers are not strategic in nature (e.g., private equity funds) or there are not enough potential strategic buyers to attract interest and competition.

- **There is an implicit assumption in binary thinking that an owner will control the timing and conditions of that ultimate sale.** If you think you will be in control for certain, don't miss Chapter 15 in this book, "10 Reasons That Businesses Change Ownership."

From the viewpoint of ownership and management transition, it is probably best to think about the strategic control level of value as something that might or could happen at an indefinite time in the future. If a company is ultimately sold at the strategic level of value, it is best if its owners have engaged in management and ownership transition planning and action well prior to the strategic sale. The results can otherwise be disappointing.

For example, consider a successful business whose owners engaged in no ownership transition planning. There was no gifting of shares to children, no transfer of ownership to key managers or employees, and the owners, say there were two of them, sold their company at a strategic price. All of the benefit of the transaction is now in both of their estates and there has been no shifting of value to children, so that wealth could be transferred to a younger generation. The key managers did not benefit from any equity ownership, and are unhappy. And both owners, who had made promises to certain charities, lost opportunities to transfer value to them on a tax-advantaged basis.

So don't let vague and binary notions about business ownership and possible future strategic values hamper management and ownership transition planning. From an ownership and management transition perspective, the strategic control value should be considered as the potential for a good payday, someday, maybe.

Financial Control Level

The financial control level of value lies in the middle of the conceptual levels of value chart. Financial control value is based on the normalized cash flows of a business, where unusual and non-recurring items and owner-related discretionary expenses are also adjusted.

When owners negotiate regarding buy-sell agreement pricing, they will normally agree on a financial control level of value as the price to be determined if their agreement is triggered. The logic flows from the examples of different values noted above. Owner A and Owner B are negotiating how the price for their buy-sell agreement is to be determined by an independent appraiser at any future valuation dates. Consider their thought processes:

- Both owners want the best possible price for them or their families if and when the agreement is triggered.

- Neither owner knows who will be the first to trigger the buy-sell agreement.

- Owner A would like a strategic price (like the $130 per share strategic price above) if he has to sell pursuant to the agreement.

- However, Owner A is concerned that if he is the buyer if Owner B triggers the agreement, he doesn't want to pay $130 per share, but rather the much lower $65 per share that is a nonmarketable level of value.

- However, Owner B would not accept a potentially discounted price of $65 per share because he might be the first to trigger the agreement.

- Both Owner A and Owner B figure out that while neither will obtain a strategic price, neither of them will get a deeply discounted price, and so they agree on reasonable pricing based at the financial control level for their buy-sell agreement.

The benefit of financial control pricing is the avoidance of uncertainty about future pricing and the assurance of the opportunity for a reasonable rate of return on their investments in the event there is a future trigger event.

Similarly, the financial control level of value is often employed for pricing when owners sell their shares back to a business, either partially or in total. This is certainly the case when existing owners have negotiating leverage. The benefits of leveraged share repurchases to remaining owners are discussed in detail in Chapters 9 and 10 of this book.

Some owners who have control of a business think that their controlling interests are worth more than the interests of minority shareholders. That may be true in the world of fair market value, which is a willing buyer and willing seller world. However, it may be difficult to employ in the real world, particularly if noncontrolling owners have leverage, e.g., like holding key management positions. All owners in a business, either controlling or noncontrolling, should be entitled to receive reasonable returns for their investments.

Perhaps that is a value judgment on my part, but the financial control level of value is often perceived to be the most reasonable for transactions that occur in the interim between now and any ultimate sale or disposition of a business. That's the conclusion of the great majority of states when controlling owners engage in transactions that provide dissenting shareholder rights to affected minority owners. The same is generally true in cases of shareholder oppression by controlling owners of a business.

Statutory fair value determinations are required in most states, either based on statute or judicial interpretation, at controlling interest levels of value where minority and controlling owners are to achieve similar values, and neither minority interest nor marketability discounts are allowed.

From the viewpoint of ownership and management transition, the financial control level of value is a good starting point. It is the most likely level of value to be agreed upon in buy-sell agreements and for many other internal ownership transactions for closely held and family businesses and their owners.

Nonmarketable Minority (Discounted) Level of Value

The nonmarketable minority level of value sits at the bottom of the conceptual levels of value chart in Figure 7.

We defined fair market value above. Fair market value at the nonmarketable minority level is an appraisal construct based on current tax law. Appraisers attempt to mirror the negotiations of hypothetical investors engaging in transactions involving illiquid minority interests of businesses. Values are determined based on the relative attractiveness of the investment to both buyers and sellers and on the specific investment characteristics of the investment being valued.

Marketability discounts reflect the diminished attractiveness of illiquid interests relative to marketable interests (marketable minority, or as-if-freely-tradable, or financial control where an entire company is marketed). Value for such interests are based on the normalized cash flows of a business. Cash flows for minority interests are usually less than the cash flows of the enterprise and illiquid minority interests are perceived as carrying higher risks than the risks of their related enterprises. They also generally have potentially long and indeterminate expected holding periods. These adverse factors give rise to what is called the marketability discount.

For these reasons, in fair market value determinations, it is typical to apply marketability discounts from marketable minority/financial control base values based on the analysis of the appraisers.

The significance of this pertains to gift and estate tax planning. Consider the following example:

- Assume that a company has 100,000 shares outstanding and a financial control value of $100 per share. The financial control value equity, a proxy for marketable minority value, is therefore $10 million.

- Now assume that an owner wants to gift $1.0 million of value to a child. At the financial control value of $100 per share, he would be able to gift 10,000 shares to the child, or a 10.0% economic interest.

- Now further assume that the nonmarketable minority is $65 per share as noted above. The same owner could make a gift of about 15,400 shares, or 15.4% of the company, for the same dollar gift amount of $1.0 million.

Under current tax law in the United States, if the gift were supported by an appropriate appraisal, this larger gift would be perfectly allowable. The significance of early gifting, if that is an owner's intent can be overlooked or misunderstood. In the example we are just describing, and forgetting any issues related to timing:

- The $1.0 million gift at financial control would be worth $1.3 million at an assumed strategic control value of $130 per share.

- The same $1.0 million gift based on the nonmarketable minority value of $65 per share, yielding a gift of 15.4 thousand shares, would be worth $2.0 million at the assumed strategic control value of $130 per share.

Clearly, there is potential for shifting value between generations through careful gift and estate tax planning. This topic is well beyond the scope of this book, but appropriate planning between now and any ultimate sale or disposition of your business is an important aspect of employing *The One Percent Solution* to manage your private company wealth.

From the viewpoint of ownership and management transition, the non-marketable minority value is primarily associated with gift and estate tax planning. Charitable gifts are made under the same fair market standard, as well.

Concluding Thoughts

We have walked through the levels of value and related them to the kind of transactions they represent and the kinds of ownership transition activities they facilitate. We can summarize the discussion as follows:

- **Strategic Control Value.** This conceptual value relates to hypo-thetical transactions involving strategic, or synergistic buyers. Unless typical buyers are strategic in nature, the strategic con-trol level is not a normal fair market value concept. For business owners, the strategic level represents a potential, higher value that might be available some day at an indeterminate time in the future. Business owners should not let thoughts of poten-tial future strategic values interfere with normal ownership and management transition activities.

- **Financial Control Value (Marketable Minority).** Financial control value is a fair market value concept on an enterprise basis. It is often considered as the appropriate level of value for buy-sell agreements and many other internal transactions involving closely held and family business ownership interests.

- **Nonmarketable Minority Level.** This conceptual level of value is associated with gift and estate tax planning. It is a discounted level of value that considers the potential unattractiveness of illiquid minority investments from the viewpoint of owners who might be "outside the family" in closely held and family businesses. This allowable level of value for gift and estate tax purposes facilitates the shifting of value between generations if appropriately employed.

The value of your business is a range concept. Good estate planning calls for transferring business value at discounted prices so that at future dates, the next generation(s) can benefit by receiving undiscounted, and perhaps, strategic pricing upon an ultimate sale or dissolution. Financial control is the level most often agreed upon between fellow owners as the most reasonable pricing for buy-sell agreements and other internal transactions.

The management of your private company wealth will benefit from your understanding and use of these levels of value concepts will facilitate the management of your private company wealth if you put them to practical use between now and any ultimate sale or disposition of your business or your interest in a closely held of family business.

Tools for Managing Private Company Wealth

CHAPTER 7

Strategy Options for Managing Private Wealth

A number of *One Percent Solution* activities were identified in the previous chapter, including wealth manager compensation, annual appraisals for monitoring performance, buy-sell agreement pricing, life insurance funding, estate planning, and others. It is now time to identify a number of *One Percent Solution* strategies for managing private wealth.

Liquidity and Diversification Without Selling

As noted earlier, business owners often think of ownership in binary fashion: "Either I own the business, or I don't. I'll just keep it until I sell it, and that's that." However, it is a fact that every business owner will sell his or her business, either partially or totally and these sales will occur voluntarily or involuntarily.

Consider again the options in the Ownership Transfer Matrix as shown in Figure 8.

The Ownership Transfer Matrix identifies many of the things that can or will happen to cause owners of closely held businesses to sell some or all of their investments.

The Ownership Transfer Matrix

	Partial Sale/Transfer	Total Sale/Transfer
Voluntary Transfer	ESOP Outside Investor(s) Sales to Insiders/Relatives Combination Merger/Cash Out Going Public Gifting Programs Buy-Sell Agreements	Sale of Business Stock-for-Stock Exchange with Public Company Stock Cash Sale to Public Company Installment Sale to Relatives/Insiders ESOP/Management Buyout Liquidation Buy-Sell Agreements
Involuntary Transfer	Death Divorce Forced Restructuring Shareholder Disputes Buy-Sell Agreements	Death Divorce Forced Restructuring Bankruptcy Shareholder Disputes Liquidation Buy-Sell Agreements

Figure 8

As briefly discussed in Chapter 3, there is no way out of the boxes. Many owners of interests in closely held or family businesses may sell or transfer portions of their interests, either willingly (like in gifting programs) or unwillingly (as in a forced redemption in a shareholder dispute).

Every owner of an interest in a business will sell or transfer his or her entire interest, if only at the time of death. As they say, "You can't take it with you!"

Owners who follow *The One Percent Solution* will be working with appropriate advisers to make conscious decisions regarding partial sales or transfers during their lifetimes. Reasons include sales of partial interests to diversify ownership and net worth, gifting of stock to family members, sales of stock to insiders, or members of the management team, and others.

Owners who follow *The One Percent Solution* will sometimes plan to sell their entire interests in their companies. This could mean selling the entire company on a planned basis, or selling a particular owner's entire interest to the company, other shareholders, or outside owners (like private equity firms or other capable investors with interests in illiquid assets).

A number of financial tools are available to the typical, successful closely held or family business to assist in the investment management objectives of creating liquidity, diversifying wealth, reducing risk, and enhancing returns.

A number of financial tools are available to the typical, successful closely held or family business to assist in the investment management objectives of creating liquidity, diversifying wealth, reducing risk, and enhancing returns.

Unfortunately many of these tools are overlooked not only by business owners, but by their advisers as well. The tools are of no use to owners who do not use them while they can be used. By now you know we mean between your current status quo and any ultimate sale or disposition of your business.

Corporate Finance Strategies/Tools for Private Businesses

There are legitimate, effective, and available alternative techniques to create shareholder liquidity and cash flow, enhance business performance and returns, and provide opportunities for overall portfolio diversification. Not all of these will be appropriate for all companies at all times, but they all may be appropriate for consideration under specific conditions and circumstances.

Status Quo	Easily Implemented Options	Significant & Realistic Minority Options	Control-Level Options	Third-Party Sale (Financial/Strategic)
	Regular dividends	Leveraged dividend recap *(say 30% or less)*	Leveraged dividend recap *(say 50-60% or more)*	
	Special dividend	Leveraged stock recap (buy-back) *(say 30% or less)*	Leveraged stock recap (buy-back) *(say 50-60% or more)*	
	Repurchase shares from owners desiring to sell	Employee stock ownership plan *(say 30% or less)*	Employee stock ownership plan *(say 50-60% or more)*	
	Establish a management buy-in program	Non-control private equity investment for liquidity/growth	Private equity (majority investment)	

Figure 9

The "bookends" chart in Figure 9 briefly outlines three levels of wealth management strategies for private businesses, all of which are available to most companies between now and any ultimate disposition. None of the options requires a sale of the business.

- Easily implemented options include dividend policy and occasional share repurchases.

- Significant minority options include leveraged dividend recapitalizations and leveraged share repurchases.

- Control level options may cede control to others while maintaining significant ownership.

The various strategies provide shareholder benefits, including:

- Enhancement of returns on equity.

- Enhancement in earnings per share.

- Acceleration of cash returns.

- Enhanced performance and reduced business risk.

- Optimization of capital structures of companies.

- Liquidity for shareholders independent of their companies.

- Ability for shareholders to diversify their portfolios.

We examine these options in greater detail in Figure 10 on the following pages.

The techniques work for others and they can work for you.

Using *One Percent Solution* strategies is tantamount to applying basic tools of corporate finance to private corporate America. These tools are not the sole province of public companies and private equity funds. The tools work for others, and they can work for you.

	Owner Options	Benefits of Strategy	Risks/Other Considerations
1	Status Quo	• Grow revenues and earnings • Benefit from future appreciation (at risk of value declining) • Maintain control for existing controller(s) • Maintain ownership status quo	• Face execution risk of growth strategy • Absence of liquidity and ownership transition • May not advance necessary management transitions • Needs to be a conscious decision and not based on procrastination
Easily Implemented Options			
2	Regular Dividends	• Current returns to shareholders • Initial step toward diversification • Enhance capital structure and maintain return on equity	• Little downside risk if attractive reinvestment opportunities are not available • Focuses management attention on maintaining regular dividend • Enhances attractiveness of minority ownership interests • Paid to shareholders pro rata • Does not change or facilitate ownership transition
3	Special Dividend	• Liquidity to shareholders from excess assets • Potential diversification opportunity • Enhance capital structure and return on equity	• Paid to shareholders pro rata • Does not change or facilitate ownership transition
4	Repurchase Shares from Owners Desiring to Sell	• Generally small transactions • Use excess assets, seller financing or external financing • Liquidity opportunity for selling shareholder(s) • Enhanced returns/relative ownership % for remaining owners	• Easy to accomplish • Must establish/agree on pricing • Favorable dividend treatment for selling owner(s) • Makes a partial market in shares and enhances attractiveness of minority ownership • Reasonable transaction costs
5	Establish a Management Buy-in Program	• Helps to align interests of key managers with company • Installment sale can facilitate transition • Effect with treasury stock and dilute other owners • Effect with sales by other owners (liquidity for them)	• Pricing and terms should be reasonable so that purchases can be reasonably paid for • Creeping sales, and often not possible in large amounts (% of company) • Can facilitate both ownership and management transitions

Figure 10

Owner Options	Benefits of Strategy	Risks/Other Considerations
Significant and Realistic Minority Options		
6 Leveraged Dividend Recap (Minority, say 30% or less)	• Potentially significant diversification opportunity • Enhance capital structure and return on equity • Perhaps good in conjunction with "status quo" strategy • Shift risk from equity owners to lenders	• Little downside if leverage is not excessive • External lenders will require certain restrictive financial covenants • Tax on dividends at dividend rate
7 Leveraged Stock Recap (Buy-Back) (Minority, say 30% or less)	• Creates liquidity and diversification opportunities • Capital gains treatment for selling shareholder(s) • Enhanced ROE for remaining owners • Optimize capital structure • Dividend pick-up if company pays and maintains a dividend • Enhanced ownership percentages for remaining owners • Can facilitate ownership transition	• Reasonable risk of leverage is not excessive • External lenders will require certain restrictive financial covenants • Potential for change of control depending on ownership structure • Price will be a financial price (rather than strategic) • Reasonable transaction costs
8 Employee Stock Ownership Plan (Minority, say 30% or less)	• Creates liquidity and diversification opportunities • Selling shareholder (controller) defines process • Ownership incentive for employees • Can be part of ownership and management transition • Potentially favorable tax treatment on rollover investments	• ESOP legal and regulatory complexities • Potential to increase risk for employee retirement if replace profit sharing or other plan(s) • Potential fairness issues to be addressed • Price will be financial (not strategic) • Company will have ongoing repurchase obligation (manageable in most cases) • Expectation of significant management consistency • Reasonable transaction costs • ESOP transactions are usually 100% • Personal guaranties will likely be required by lenders from selling owners
9 Non-Control Private Equity Investment for Liquidity/ Growth	• Growing pool of capital for minority interest investment • Pricing typically financial in nature • Bring on new owners with business/transaction experience • Source of partial liquidity while maintaining control	• Private Equity (P/E) owners may require enhanced discipline and accountability • P/E owners will seek liquidity in 5 to 7 years • P/E owners will require elements of control even with minority investments

Figure 10

	Owner Options	Benefits of Strategy	Risks/Other Considerations
Control-Level Options			
10	Leveraged Dividend Recap (Majority, say 50% to 60% of value)	• Potentially significant diversification opportunity • Enhance capital structure and return on equity • Perhaps good in conjunction with "status quo" strategy • Shift risk from equity owners to lenders	• More downside with greater leverage than for smaller transaction • External lenders will require certain restrictive financial covenants • Could require more expensive non-bank lenders • Tax on dividends at dividend rate
11	Leveraged Stock Recap (Buy-Back) (Majority, up to 50% to 60%)	• Accelerates ownership transition and change of control • Facilitates ownership transition • Management transition may be part of process • Same benefit as prior option	• More risk for remaining owners with higher leverage with larger transaction • External lenders will require certain restrictive financial covenants • Potential solvency issues to be addressed • Change of control is likely goal • Price will be financial (rather than strategic) • Reasonable transaction costs, but likely higher than above • Remaining owners provide equity portion of financing
12	Employee Stock Ownership Plan (ESOP, up to 50% to 60%)	• Creates liquidity and diversification opportunities • Selling shareholder (controller) defines process • Ownership incentive for employees • Can be part of ownership and management transition	• ESOP legal and regulatory has complexities • Potential to increase risk for employee retirement if replace profit sharing or other plan(s) • Potential fairness issues to be addressed • Price will be financial (not strategic) • Company will have ongoing repurchase obligation (manageable in most cases) • Expectation of significant management consistency • Reasonable transaction costs • ESOP is fully leveraged • Personal guaranties required by lenders from selling owners
13	Private Equity (Majority Investment)	• Creates liquidity and diversification opportunities • Facilitates ownership transition • Management transition may be part of process • Selling owners may be required to retain equity in business • Equity retention provides upside but risk, as well	• Private equity (P/E) may change ownership/management dynamics • Growth capital (leverage) may be part of deal • P/E investors will have control • External lenders will require certain restrictive financial covenants

Figure 10

Owner Options	Benefits of Strategy	Risks/Other Considerations
Third-Party Sale Options		
14 Third-Party Sale (Financial Buyer)	• Total liquidity for owners and diversification opportunities • Completes ownership transition • May retain management positions for key managers	• Price is financial (not strategic) • Choice re timing of transaction if performance is good • Should be conscious, long-term plan • All planned gift/estate tax planning should be completed in advance • Watch out for requested owner financing • Some choice over potential purchasers to approach • Transaction costs include transaction adviser, counsel, etc.
15 Third-Party Sale (Strategic Buyer)	• Total liquidity for owners and diversification opportunities • Completes ownership transition	• Only option where strategic price is available (if there is competition) • How is the economy, the stock market, and industry performing? • What is the company's unique brand or competitive position? • Don't bet on long-term employment with new buyer • Social costs of integration and financial costs of potential loss of jobs • Potential for partial consideration in stock of public or private acquirer

Figure 10

67

CHAPTER 8

An Introduction to Dividends and Dividend Policy for Private Companies

The issue of dividends and dividend policy is of great significance to owners of closely held and family businesses and deserves considered attention.

Fortunately, I had an early introduction to dividend policy beginning with a call from a client back in the 1980s.

I had been valuing a family business, Plumley Rubber Company, founded by Mr. Harold Plumley, for a number of years. One day in the latter 1980s, Mr. Plumley called me and asked me to help him establish a formal dividend policy for his company, which was owned by himself and his four sons, all of whom worked in the business.

Normally I do not divulge the names of clients, but my association with the Plumley family and Plumley Companies (its later name) was made public in 1996 when Michael Plumley, oldest son of the founder and then President of the company, spoke at the 1996 International Business Valuation Conference of the American Society of Appraisers held in Memphis, Tennessee. He told the story of Plumley Companies and was kind enough to share a portion of my involvement with them over nearly 20 years at that point.

Let's put dividends into perspective, beginning with a discussion of (net) earnings and (net) cash flow. These are two very important concepts for any discussion about dividends and dividend policy for closely held and family businesses. To simplify, I'll often drop the (net) when discussion earnings and cash flow, but you will see that this little word is important.

(Net) Earnings of a Business

The earnings of a business can be expressed by the simple equation:

$$Earnings = Total\ Revenue - Total\ Cost$$

Costs include all the operating costs of a business, including taxes.

- **C Corporations.** If your corporation is a C corporation, it will pay taxes on its earnings and earnings will be net of taxes. The line on the income statement is that of net income, or the income remaining after all expenses, including taxes, both state and federal, have been paid. By the way, if your company is a C corporation, feel free to give me a call to start a conversation about this decision.

- **S Corporations and LLCs.** If your corporation is an S corporation or an LLC (limited liability company), the company will make a distribution so that its owners can pay their pass-through taxes on the income. To get to the equivalent point of net income on a C corporation's income statement, it is necessary to go to the line called net income (but it is not) and to subtract the total amount of distributions paid to owners for them to pay the state and federal income taxes they owe on the company's (i.e., their pass through) earnings. This amount would come from the cash flow statement or the statement of changes in retained earnings.

Ignoring any differences in tax rates, the net income, after taxes (corporate or personal) should be about the same for C corporations and pass-through entities.

(Net) Cash Flow

Companies have non-cash charges like depreciation and amortization related to fixed assets and intangible assets. They also have cash charges for things that don't flow through the income statement. Capital expenditures for plant and equipment, buildings, computers and other fixed assets are netted against depreciation and amortization, and the result is either positive or negative in a given year. Capital expenditures tend to be "lumpy" while the related depreciation expenses are amortized over a period of years, often causing swings in the net of the two.

There are other "expenses" and "income" of businesses that do not flow through the income statement. These investments, either positive or negative, relate to the working capital of a business. Working capital assets include inventories and accounts receivable, and working capital liabilities include accounts payable and other short-term obligations. Changes in working capital can lead to a range of outcomes for a business. Consider these two extremes that could occur regarding cash in a given year:

We focus on cash flow because it is the source of all good things that come from a business.

- **Make lots of money but have no cash.** Rapidly growing companies may find that while they have positive earnings, they have no cash left at the end of the month or year. They have to finance their rapid growth by leaving all or more than all of earnings in the business in the form of working capital to finance investments in accounts receivable and/or inventories and in the purchase of fixed assets to support that growth.

- **Make little money, even have losses, and generate cash.** Companies that experience sales declines may earn little, or even lose money on the income statement, and still generate lots of cash because they collect prior receivables or convert previously accumulated inventories into cash during the slowdown.

Working capital on the balance sheet is the difference between current assets and current liabilities. Many companies have short-term lines of credit with which they finance working capital investments. The concept of working capital, then, may include changes in short-term debt.

In addition, companies generate cash by borrowing funds on a longer-term basis, for example, to finance lumpy capital expenditures. In the course of a year, a company may be a net borrower of long-term debt or be in a position of paying down its long-term debt. So we'll need to consider the net change in long-term debt if we want to understand what happens to cash in a business during a given year.

We are developing a concept of (net) cash flow, which can be defined as follows in Figure 11.

Most financial analysts and bankers will agree that this is a pretty good definition of Net Cash Flow.

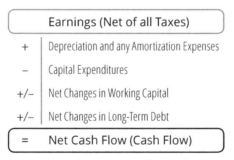

	Earnings (Net of all Taxes)
+	Depreciation and any Amortization Expenses
−	Capital Expenditures
+/−	Net Changes in Working Capital
+/−	Net Changes in Long-Term Debt
=	Net Cash Flow (Cash Flow)

Figure 11

Net Cash Flow is the Source of Good Things

We focus on cash flow because it is the source of all good things that come from a business. The current year's cash flow for a business is, for example, the source of:

- **Long-term debt repayment.** Paying debt is good. Bankers are extremely focused on cash flow, because they only want to lend long-term funds to businesses that have the expectation of sufficient cash flow to repay the debt, including principal and interest on the scheduled basis. Interest expense has already been paid when we look at net cash flow. Companies borrow on a long-term basis to finance a number of things like land, buildings and equipment, software and hardware, and many other productive assets that may be difficult to finance currently. They may also borrow on a long term basis to finance stock repurchases or special dividends.

- **Reinvestment for future growth.** Investment in a business is good if adequate returns are available. If a company generates positive cash flow in a given year, it is available to reinvest in the business to finance its future growth. Reinvested earnings are a critical source of investment capital for closely held and private companies Reinvesting with the expectation of future growth (in dividends and capital gains) is an important source of shareholder returns, but the return is deferred, at least in the form of cash, until a future date.

- **Dividends or distributions.** Corporate dividends are also good, particularly if you are a recipient. Cash flow is also the normal source for dividends (for C corporation owners) or what we call "economic distributions," or distributions net of shareholder pass-through taxes (for S corporation and LLC owners).

What is a Dividend?

At its simplest, a dividend (or economic distribution) reflects the portion of earnings not reinvested in a business in a given year, but paid out to owners in the form of current returns.

For some or many closely held and family businesses, effective dividends can include another component, and that is the amount of any discretionary expenses that likely would be "normalized" if they were to be sold. Discretionary expenses include:

- **Above-market compensation for owner-managers.** Owners of some private businesses who compensate themselves and/or family members at above-market rates should realize that the above-market portion of such compensation is an effective dividend.

- **Mystery employees on the payroll.** Some companies place non-working spouses, children or other relatives on the payroll when no work is required of them.

- **Expenses associated with non-operating assets used for owners' personal benefit.** Non-operating assets can include company-owned vacation homes, aircraft not necessary for the operation of the business, vehicles operated by non-working family members, and others.

It is essential to analyze above-market compensation and other discretionary expenses from owners' viewpoints to ascertain the real rate of return that is obtained from investments in private businesses. In an earlier chapter, we touched on the concept of the rate of return on investment for a closely held business. Assuming that there were no realized capital gains from a business during a given year, the annual return (AR) is measured as follows:

$$AR = \frac{(\text{Dividends} + \text{Unrealized Appreciation})}{\text{Beginning Portfolio Balance}}$$

Now, we add to this any discretionary expenses that are above market or not normal operating expenses of the business that are taken out by owners:

$$AR = \frac{\left(\text{Dividends} + \begin{array}{c}\text{Discretionary}\\\text{Benefits}\end{array} + \begin{array}{c}\text{Unrealized}\\\text{Appreciation}\end{array}\right)}{\text{Beginning Value of a Business}}$$

We now know what dividends are, and they include discretionary benefits that will likely be ceased and normalized into earnings in the event of a sale.

We won't focus on discretionary benefits in the continuing discussion of dividends and dividend policy. However, it is important for business owners to understand that, to the extent discretionary benefits exist, they reflect portions of their returns on investments in their businesses.

In summary, dividends are current returns to the owners of a business. Dividends are normally residual payments to owners after all other necessary debt obligations have been paid and all desirable reinvestments in the business have been made.

Dividends and Dividend Policy for Private Companies

With the above introduction to dividends for private companies, we can now talk about dividend policy. The remainder of this chapter focuses on seven critical things for consideration as you think about your company's dividend policy.

1. Every company has a dividend policy.

2. Dividend policy influences return on business investment.

3. Dividend policy is a starting point for portfolio diversification.

4. Special dividends enhance personal liquidity and diversification.

5. Dividend policy does matter for private companies.

6. Dividend policy focuses management attention on financial performance.

7. Boards of directors need to establish thoughtful dividend policies.

We now focus on each of these seven factors you need to know about your company's dividend policy.

Every Company Has a Dividend Policy

Let's begin with the obvious observation that your company has a dividend policy. It may not be a formal policy, but you have one. Every year, every company earns money (or not) and generates cash flow (or not). Assume for the moment that a company generates positive earnings as we defined the term above. If you think about it, there are only three things that can be done with the earnings of a business:

- Reinvest the earnings in the business, either in the form of working capital, plant and equipment, software and computers, and the like, or even excess or surplus assets.

- Pay down debt.

- Pay dividends to owners (or economic distributions – after pass-through taxes – for S corporations and LLCs) or repurchase stock (another form of returns to shareholders).

That's it. Those are all the choices. Every business will do one or more of these things with its earnings each year. If a business generates excess cash and reinvests in CDs, or accumulates other non-operating assets, it is reinvesting in the business, although likely not at an optimal rate of return on the reinvestment. Even if your business does not pay a dividend to you and your fellow owners, you have a dividend policy and your dividend payout ratio is 0% of earnings.

On the other hand, if your business generates substantial cash flow and does not require significant reinvestment to grow, it may be possible to have a dividend policy of paying out 90% or even up to 100% of earnings in most years. This is often the case in non capital intensive service businesses.

Recall that if a business pays discretionary benefits to its owners that are above market rates of compensation, or if it pays significant expenses that are personal to the owners, it is the economic equivalent of paying a dividend to owners. So when talking to business owners where such expenses are significant, we remind them that they are, indeed, paying dividends and should be aware of that fact.

Some may think that discretionary expenses are the provenance of only small businesses; however, they exist in many businesses of substantial size, even into the hundreds of millions in value.

Discretionary expenses are not necessarily bad, but they can create issues. In companies with more than one shareholder, discretionary expenses create the potential for (un)fairness issues. However, discretionary expenses are paid for the benefit of one shareholder or group of shareholders and not for others, they are still a return to some shareholders.

Every company, including yours, has a dividend policy. Is it the right policy for your company and its owners?

Dividend Policy Influences Return on Business Investment

To see the relationship between dividend policy and return on investment we can examine a couple of equations. This brief discussion is based on a lengthier discussion in my book, *Business Valuation: An Integrated Theory Second Edition* (John Wiley & Sons, 2007). There is a basic valuation equation, referred to as the Gordon Model. This model states that the price (P_0) of a security is its expected dividend (D_1) capitalized at its discount rate (R) minus its expected long term growth rate in the dividend (G_d). This model is expressed as follows:

$$P_0 = \frac{D_1}{(R-G_d)}$$

D_1 is equal to Earnings times the portion of earnings paid out, or the dividend payout ratio (DPO), so we can rewrite the basic equation as follows:

$$P_0 = \frac{\text{Earnings x DPO}}{(R-G_d)}$$

What this equation says is that the more that a company pays out in dividends, the less rapidly it will be able to grow, because Gd, or the growth rate in the dividend, is actually the expected growth rate of earnings based on the relevant dividend policy.

We can look at this simplistically in word equations as follows:

Dividend Income + Capital Gains = Total Return

Dividend Yield + Growth (Appreciation) = Cost of Equity (or the discount rate, R)

These equations reflect basic corporate finance principles that pertain, not only to public companies, but to private businesses as well. There is an important assumption in all of the above equations – cash flow not paid out in dividends is reinvested in the business at its discount rate, R.

There are many examples of successful private companies that do not pay dividends, even in the face of unfavorable reinvestment opportunities. To the extent that dividends are not paid and earnings are reinvested in low-yielding assets, the accumulation of excess assets will tend to dampen the return on equity and investment returns for all shareholders.

Further, the accumulation of excess assets dampens the relative valuation of companies, because return on equity (ROE) is an important driver of value. For example, consider the following relationship without proof:

ROE x Price/Earnings Multiple = Price/Book Value

At a given multiple of (net) earnings available in the marketplace, a company's ROE will determine its price/book value multiple. The price/book value multiple tells how valuable a company is in relationship to its book value, or the depreciated cost value of its shareholders' investments in the business.

Let's consider a simple example. Assume that a company generates an ROE of 10% and that the relevant market price/earnings multiple (P/E) is 10x. Using the formula above:

Price/Book Value	=	ROE x P/E
	=	10% x 10
	=	100%

In this example, the company would be valued at its book value and the shareholders would not benefit from any "goodwill," or value in excess of book value. Consider, however, that a similar company earns an ROE of 15%.

- Assuming the same P/E of 10x, it would be valued at 150% of its book value.

- Suppose the second company, because of its superior returns, received a P/E of 11x. In that case the price/book multiple would be 165%.

To the extent that a company's dividend policy influences its ongoing ROE, it influences its relative value in the marketplace and the ongoing returns its shareholders receive.

In short, your dividend policy influences your return on investment in your business, as well as your current returns from that investment.

Dividend Policy is a Starting Point for Portfolio Diversification

Recall the story of my being asked to help develop a dividend policy for a private company. The company had grown rapidly for a number of years and its growth and diversification opportunities in the auto parts supply business were not as attractive as they had been. The CEO, who was the majority shareholder, realized this and also that his sons (his fellow shareholders) could benefit from a current return on their investments in the company, which, collectively, were significant.

We reviewed the dividend policies of all of the public companies that we believed to be reasonably comparable to the company. I don't recall the exact numbers now, but I believe that the average dividend yield for the public companies was in the range of 3%. As I analyzed the private company, it was clear that it was still growing somewhat faster than the publics, so the ultimate recommendation for a dividend was about 1.5% of value.

The value that the 1.5% dividend yield was compared to was the independent appraisal that we prepared each year. Based on the value at the time, I recall that the annual dividend began at something on the order of $300,000 per year. But, for the father and the sons, it was a beginning point for diversification of their portfolios away from total concentration in their successful private business.

Your dividend policy can be the starting point for wealth diversification, or it can enhance the diversification process if it is already underway.

Special Dividends Enhance Personal Liquidity and Diversification

A number of years ago, I was an adviser to a publicly traded bank holding company. Because of past anemic dividends, this bank had accumulated several million dollars of excess capital. The stock was very thinly traded and the market price was quite low, reflecting a very low ROE (remember the discussion above).

Because of the very thin market for shares, a stock repurchase program was not considered workable. After some analysis, I recommended that the board of directors approve a large, one-time special dividend. At the same time I suggested they approve a small increase in the ongoing quarterly dividend. Both of these recommendations provided shareholders with liquidity and the opportunity to diversify their holdings.

Since the board of directors collectively held a large portion of the stock, the discussion of liquidity and diversification opportunities while maintaining their relative ownership position in the bank was attractive.

At the final board meeting before the transaction, one of the directors did a little bit of math. He noted that if they paid out a large special dividend, the bank would lose earnings on those millions and earnings would decline. I agreed with his math, but pointed out (calculations already in the board package) that the assets being liquidated were very low in yield and that earnings (and earnings per share) would not decline much. With equity being reduced by a larger percentage, the bank's ROE should increase. So that increase in ROE, given a steady P/E multiple in the marketplace, should increase the bank's Price/Book Value multiple.

The director put me on the spot. He asked point blank: "What will happen to the stock price?" I told him that I didn't know for sure (does one ever?) but that it should increase somewhat and, if the markets believed that they would operate similarly in the future, it could increase a good bit. The stock price increased more than 20% following the special dividend.

Special dividends, to the extent that your company has excess assets, can enhance personal liquidity and diversification. They can also help increase ongoing shareholder returns. I have always been against retaining significant excess assets on company balance sheets because of their negative effect on shareholder returns and their adverse psychological impact. It is too easy for management to get "comfortable" with a bloated balance sheet.

If your business has excess assets, consider paying a special dividend. Your shareholders will appreciate it.

Dividend Policy Does Matter for Private Companies

Someone once said that earnings are a matter of opinion, but dividends are a matter of fact. What we know is that when dividends are paid, the owners of companies enjoy their benefit, pay their taxes, and make individual choices regarding their reinvestment or consumption.

The total return from an investment in a business equals its dividend yield plus appreciation (assuming no capital gains), relative to beginning value. However, unlike unrealized appreciation, returns from dividends are current and bankable. They reduce the uncertainty of achieving returns. Further, if a company's growth has slowed because of relatively few good reinvestment opportunities, a healthy dividend policy can help assure continuing favorable returns overall.

Based on many years of working with closely held businesses, we have observed that companies that do not pay dividends and, instead, accumulate excess assets, tend to have lower returns over time. There is, however, a more insidious issue. The management of companies that maintain lots of excess assets may tend to get lazy-minded. Worse, however, is the opposite tendency. With lots of cash on hand, it is too easy to feel pressure to make a large and perhaps unwise investment, e.g., an acquisition, that will not only consume the excess cash but detract from returns in the remainder of the business.

Dividend policy is the throttle by which well-run companies gauge their speed of reinvestment. If investment opportunities abound, then a no- or low-dividend payout may be appropriate. However, if reinvestment opportunities are slim, then a heavy dividend payout may be entirely appropriate.

Any way you cut it, dividend policy does matter for private companies.

Dividend Policy Focuses Management Attention on Financial Performance

Boards of directors are generally cautious with dividends and once regular dividends are being paid, are reluctant to cut them. The need, based on declared policy, to pay out, say, 35% of earnings in the form of shareholder dividends (example only) will focus management's attention on generating sufficient earnings and cash flow each year to pay the dividend and to make necessary reinvestments in the business to keep it growing.

No management (even if it is you) wants to have to tell a board of directors (even if you are on it) or shareholder group that the dividend may need to be reduced or eliminated because of poor financial performance.

Boards of Directors Need to Establish Thoughtful Dividend Policies

If dividend policy is the throttle with which to manage cash flow not needed for reinvestment in a business, it makes sense to handle that throttle carefully and thoughtfully. Returns to shareholders can come in the form of dividends or in the form of share repurchases.

While a share repurchase is not a cash dividend, it does provide cash to selling shareholders and offsetting benefits to remaining shareholders. Chapter 10 of the book (Leveraged Share Repurchase: An Illustrative Example) provides an example of a substantial leveraged share repurchase from a controlling shareholder to provide liquidity and diversification.

From a theoretical and practical standpoint, the primary reason to withhold available dividends today is to reinvest to be able to provide larger future dividends – and larger in present value terms today. It is not a good dividend policy to withhold dividends for reasons like the following:

- A patriarch *withholds dividends* to prevent the second (or third or more) generations from being able to have access to funds.

- A control group chooses to *defer dividends* to avoid making distributions to certain minority shareholders.

- Dividends are *not paid* because management (and the board) want to build a large nest egg against possible future adversities.

- Dividends are *not paid* to accumulate excess or non-operating assets on the balance sheet for personal or vanity reasons.

Dividend policy is important and your board of directors needs to establish a thoughtful dividend policy for your business.

Dividends and dividend policies are important for the owners of closely held and family businesses. Dividends can provide a source of liquidity and diversification for owners of private companies. Dividend policy can also have an impact on the way that management focuses on financial performance.

CHAPTER 9

Leveraged Dividends and Leveraged Share Repurchases

In this chapter, we provide an overview of leveraged dividend recapitalizations and leveraged share repurchases. We set up a concrete example and discuss the rationale for one company's decision to engage in a leveraged share repurchase. In the next chapter, we examine the details of the transaction we introduce here.

The Situation

William co-founded Acme Company (the Company) more than thirty years ago. Since then, the Company has grown to become a $250 million business that manufactures and distributes a wide range of products for the extraction industries. William's original partner left the business more than a decade ago and his shares were acquired by the Company and a group of senior managers, including William's son, Robert.

William is interested in leaving the Company to begin working for a local non-profit organization that he has supported financially for many years. The organization has created a full-time role for him as a development officer that is open for him at any time. William knows it is in his and the Company's best interest for him to retire, and now that he has created a place for productive involvement and engagement, he is ready for a change.

A good management team is in place at the Company, but William's over-involvement has not allowed them to manage to their capabilities. The Company has experienced declining ROE over the last few years, as attractive reinvestment opportunities have not been available. Despite a regular dividend, the Company has also been accumulating excess cash on its balance sheet.

The question for William, the Company, and its shareholders is the nature of a transaction to provide liquidity for William and potential benefits for everyone else. Two basic alternatives surfaced in the discussions.

- **Leveraged Dividend Recapitalization.** A leveraged dividend recapitalization would provide significant liquidity to William and to the remaining owners, as well. However, a leveraged dividend transaction would leave William owning 30% of the stock. The other owners, including Robert, felt that this alternative would keep William too tied to the Company, and they suggested a second alternative.

- **Engage in a Leveraged Share Repurchase.** The other shareholders believed that it would be better to create a transaction in which the Company repurchased all of William's shares in a single transaction. While they will not achieve any liquidity in such a leveraged transaction, they have confidence in their ability to manage the Company and to repay the debt over time. They are willing to defer their opportunities for liquidity to future dates.

In the end, after discussing these options with their respective professional advisers, the decision is made to engage in a leveraged share repurchase. The mechanics of the transaction will be outlined in the next chapter in some detail. In the remainder of this chapter, we will outline the similarities and differences between leveraged dividend recapitalizations and leveraged share repurchase transactions.

Qualitative Comparisons of Leveraged Dividend Recaps and Leveraged Stock Repurchases

I do not advocate maximizing leverage for leveraged transactions for most closely held and family businesses. I do, however, suggest that reasonable leverage is a useful tool for providing liquidity and diversification opportunities and for enhancing shareholder returns from private companies.

Figure 12 summarizes the major benefits of leveraged dividend recapitalizations and leveraged stock repurchases, while touching on the risks associated with each type of transaction. For purposes of discussion, we are assuming that leveraged transactions will be engaged in carefully and with reasonable levels of new leverage.

Leveraged dividend recapitalizations and leveraged stock repurchases of similar magnitude have the same impact on companies from a financial perspective. A given amount of leverage, or incremental debt, has the same balance sheet effect for either form of transaction. Additionally, the interest expense is the same, and so the impact on reported dollar earnings is also the same.

The differences in leveraged dividend and leveraged stock repurchase transactions lie in what happens to the recipients of proceeds and their different effects on ownership composition. Note the following differences (and similarities) as we expand the discussion from Figure 12:

- **Tax Treatment of Proceeds.** Dividends are taxed at dividend rates, while share repurchases, assuming the required holding period has been met, are taxed at capital gains rates. Differences in dividend and capital gains tax notes, if any, can influence the way that some owners think about dividend versus repurchase recaps.

89

Liquidity and Diversification	Leveraged Dividend Recapitalizations	Leveraged Stock Repurchases
Means of Achieving Partial Liquidity	Yes, for all shareholders	Yes, partial or full liquidity for selling owners
Creating Diversification Opportunities	Yes, for all shareholders	Yes, for selling owners
Tax Treatment	Dividend rates	Capital gains rates
Shareholder Benefits		
Effect on Number of Shares Outstanding	No effect	Reduces shares outstanding by the amount (or %) of the leveraged repurchase
Relevant Shareholders	All shareholders (no change in ownership)	Remaining (non-selling) owners
Effect on Earnings Per Share (EPS)	Decrease (earnings lowered by interest expense)	Increase (reduction in shares offsets interest expense)
Effect on Return on Equity (ROE)	Increase (equity reduced relatively more than earnings lowered)	Increase (equity reduced relatively more than earnings lowered)
Effect on Expected Future Value Growth	Increase (as debt is repaid)	Increase (as debt is repaid)
Effect on Dividends Per Share	None (assuming any prior dividend is retained)	Increase (assuming previous dollar dividend is maintained, because of reduction in number of shares)
Effect on Price/Book (P/B) Value Ratio	Increase (equity reduced relatively more than earnings lowered)	Increase (equity reduced relatively more than earnings lowered)
Effect on Pro Rata Ownership of Company	No effect (no change in number of shares outstanding)	Increase (by number of shares owned divided by (1-% of total shares repurchased)
Additional Benefits to Company and Owners		
Effect on Capital Structure	Move toward optimizing (assuming reasonable leverage)	Move toward optimizing (assuming reasonable leverage)
Effect on Management	Should focus attention on operating so that debt can be reduced timely	Should focus attention on operating so that debt can be reduced timely

Figure 12

- **Pro Forma Shares Outstanding.** Shares remain the same following a leveraged dividend transaction, and are reduced by the amount of repurchase following leveraged share repurchases. This is obvious, but important, because while dollar earning pro forma are the same in either equivalent size transaction, earnings per share increase with leveraged share repurchases.

- **Pro Forma Ownership.** There is no change in pro rata ownership following a leveraged dividend recapitalization, because there is no change in shares outstanding. However, with a leveraged share repurchase, remaining shareholders benefit from the lower number of shares outstanding with an increase in their relative ownership of the company. For example, an owner of 10% of the stock pre-transaction would own 14.3% of the remaining shares following a 30% share repurchase transaction (10% / (1-30%)).

- **Pro Forma Dollar Value.** Following either a leveraged dividend recapitalization or a leveraged share repurchase, the market value of equity will be reduced by the amount of leverage added (or excess assets employed). The value per share will also be reduced following dividend transactions. However, the value per share following a leveraged share repurchase should remain the same, because the reduction in the number of shares offsets the overall reduced equity value.

- **Pro Forma Dollar Earnings.** Leveraged transactions have no impact on pro forma EBITDA. In both dividend and repurchase transactions, however, pre-tax and net income will be reduced by the amount of incremental interest expense, adjusted for the tax benefit of the interest expense.

- **Pro Forma Return on Equity.** Net income is reduced similarly, as just seen, but not proportionate to the reduction in equity, so ROE increases similarly for both transactions.

- **Pro Forma EPS.** Earnings per share are reduced following dividend transactions because net income is lower and the shares outstanding remain the same. Earnings per share are increased following repurchase transactions, because the number of shares is reduced less proportionately than dollar earnings.

- **Value Per Share.** Value (price) per share will be reduced following leveraged dividend recapitalizations (unless offset by price/earnings multiple expansion), because returns are received pro rata by all shareholders and leverage is increased. Value per share should remain the same following share repurchase transactions because the number of shares and the market value of equity are reduced proportionately.

- **Dividends Per Share.** Assuming there was a dividend prior to a transaction and that the dollar dividend remains the same, dividends per share will also remain the same following a dividend transaction because the number of shares remains unchanged. However, given the same dollar amount of dividends following a repurchase transaction, dividends per share for remaining shares (and shareholders) will increase by the initial dividend per share divided by (1 minus the % of shares repurchased). So, for example, if the pre-transaction dividend was $3.00 per share and the company repurchased 30% of its shares, the post-transaction dividend would be $4.29 per share ($3.00 / (1-30%))

Which Transaction is Preferable?

With all of the preceding discussion of leveraged dividend recapitalizations and leveraged share repurchases, you might be asking which one is preferable? The answer is – it depends.

In the example above, we see that William chose to do a share repurchase. It satisfied his personal objectives and since he was effectively the controlling owner, he could make that decision, although he was influenced by the desires of his fellow shareholders.

If there is no desire or need to change relative ownership, a leveraged dividend recapitalization can be an ideal transaction. Shareholders can pay their taxes and do what they desire with their net proceeds. A leveraged dividend transaction is a good way of accelerating returns to owners. In the example transaction we show a share repurchase using a combination of excess assets and new debt. The discussion above compares the results of that transaction with the results of a leveraged dividend recapitalization in qualitative terms.

> If there is no desire or need to change relative ownership, a leveraged dividend recapitalization can be an ideal transaction.

Leveraged share repurchases can accomplish a number of objectives. They can provide partial or total liquidity for selected owners while enhancing the relative ownership positions of remaining owners. It is always good to think through the ownership change potential of share repurchases such that unintended changes in ownership or control do not occur.

In the context of *The One Percent Solution*, my suggestion is that business owners consider such transactions periodically as ways to help owners diversify their wealth and to achieve intended changes in ownership structure.

Other Issues With Leveraged Transactions

Given the complexities of such leveraged transactions, owners should obtain competent legal, accounting and valuation/financial advisory advice when discussing or structuring leveraged transactions. Issues involved include:

- **Financing.** It may sound obvious, but leverage implies borrowing. With leveraged dividend transactions, the borrowing will necessarily be external. With leveraged share repurchases, selling owners can finance transactions or financing can be obtained from third parties. Financing can be straightforward bank financing, or it can become more complex, depending on the size of the transaction and the degree of leverage. In any event, business owners should obtain expert financial advisory help when arranging financing. Lending agreements will almost certainly contain performance covenants and other requirements. Loan agreements range from fairly straightforward to extremely complex. In either case competent legal advice is essential.

- **Solvency.** In large transactions relative to the size of a given company, the question of pro forma solvency may need to be addressed. If required by lenders, a solvency opinion from a qualified financial advisor may be necessary. These opinions address three critical questions, among other things: 1) Does the fair market value of a company exceed its stated and known contingent liabilities? 2) After the transaction, will the company be able to pay its obligations as they mature? 3) Is there sufficient remaining capital for the company to operate on a reasonable basis? Whether a lender requires a solvency opinion or not, business owners should be keenly interested in the answers to these questions.

- **State Law.** There may be state law requirements that counsel will have to opine about relating to capital, retained earnings, and other matters.

- **Fairness.** In some instances, boards of directors engaging in leveraged transactions may want the opinion from a qualified financial advisor that the transaction is fair, from a financial point of view, from the perspective of the remaining shareholders.

Do not be put off if some of this discussion seems to be complex in nature. Conceptually, leveraged dividend recapitalizations and leveraged share repurchases are fairly straightforward in nature. If either form of transaction seems to make sense for your owners, then they should be investigated.

Conclusion

The leverage repurchase transaction between William and his company is a direct application of corporate finance tools in the private company setting.

Public companies engage in similar transactions with frequency. While many public companies have plenty of cash with which to engage in share repurchases, they also borrow funds from time-to-time for the same purpose.

Private equity firms often engage in leveraged recapitalizations. These transactions could be leveraged dividend recapitalizations or leveraged share repurchases, depending on the circumstances. For example, in the current economic environment where private equity firms have had to delay their exits from many private company investments, they have engaged in a significant number of leveraged dividend recapitalizations to generate current returns for their limited partners, returning substantial capital to them while maintaining productive investments for longer periods.

In the private company setting, leveraged transactions often make a great deal of sense. For example, in the case above, neither William nor any of the other owners desired to sell Sample Company, which would have been quite marketable. The leveraged share repurchase is a "smart money" way to accelerate returns to William, enhance corporate performance, and augment the relative ownership and returns of all remaining owners.

In my experience, most owners of successful closely held and family businesses simply do not think about using reasonable leverage as a tool to redistribute stock ownership, provide liquidity for certain shareholders, provide special dividends, or engage in other transactions designed to provide liquidity for their owners and to enhance shareholder returns. They should.

CHAPTER 10

Leveraged Share Repurchases (Buy-Backs): An Illustrative Example

One reason many writers discuss leveraged share repurchases in general terms only is that they involve a company's current income statement and balance sheet, as well as a pro forma balance sheet and income statement. Further, to see the impact on a company and its shareholders, the changes between the existing financials and the pro forma financials must be analyzed.

This chapter presents the leveraged share repurchase introduced in the last chapter. It will bring the benefits for both a company and its owners, both selling and remaining, into clear focus.

If details and numbers are not your thing, skip to the next chapter. The qualitative benefits discussed in the last chapter are quantified in this chapter.

Leveraged share repurchases can be beneficial for a company, its selling shareholder(s), and the remaining owners:

- **Selling Owners.** Leveraged share repurchases can provide opportunities for partial or total liquidity, create a means for diversification of wealth, and provide for liquidity on a tax-advantaged capital gains basis.

- **Company and Remaining Owners.** Leveraged share repurchases can enhance a company's return on equity, increase the expected growth in value for its remaining shares, provide a dividend pickup for remaining shareholders, and enhance the price/book value multiple for its valuation. Such transactions can also serve to optimize a company's capital structure and, importantly, help to keep management attention on repaying debt and managing the company for higher returns.

We learned of these benefits in the previous chapter, in which a leveraged share repurchase was described as an alternative for personal liquidity and ownership transition.

In spite of efforts to be brief, this is a somewhat lengthy chapter. However, it is well worth reading and sharing with your fellow owners and advisers.

The example presented is meant to be as representative as possible of a real company. Think about the example and try to relate its lessons to your own company, whether larger than the example or smaller, and your personal situation.

The Situation

Acme Company (the Company) has sales for the most recent year of $250 million and manufactures and distributes a wide range of products for the extraction industries. Some of its products are branded. In spite of its significant size for a private business, the Company is a relatively small player in its overall industry. The situation, before consideration of a leveraged share repurchase, looks as follows:

- Acme Company is a profitable C corporation (that's another story), with an EBITDA margin (earnings before interest, taxes, depreciation, and amortization) of just under 10% of sales, and a net profit margin, after taxes, of 4.4% of sales. For perspective, EBITDA is $24.2 million and net income is $10.9 million.

- Return on equity for the last twelve months was 8.6%, and has been trending downward in recent years as prior leverage has been paid down and as attractive reinvestment opportunities have been limited.

- The Company has $16.4 million of interest-bearing debt, which is more than offset by $20.5 million in cash. The current ratio is 4.4x, suggesting that there is substantial liquidity on the balance sheet.

- Working capital as a percentage of sales is about 32%. For perspective, the median working capital-to-sales ratio for the public companies most similar to the Company is about 20%.

- The balance sheet is funded with $126 million of equity, which comprises 72% of assets.

- For purposes of this discussion, we have valued the equity of the Company at $149 million based on an EBITDA multiple of 6.0x, which is the median multiple for the group of comparable public companies. In arriving at this value conclusion, we have subtracted debt from the MVTC (market value of total capital) and added back the cash.

- The Company is currently paying an annual dividend totaling $3.0 million, which represents a dividend payout ratio (from net income) of 27.5%. The dividend has been at or near this level for several years.

Based on this description, and the financial analysis that made it possible, Acme Company is an attractive candidate for a leveraged share repurchase transaction. William, the co-founding shareholder, owns 30% of the 1.0 million shares outstanding and has agreed to sell his shares back to the Company and to retire. He is willing to sell his stake to the Company if a reasonable transaction – for him and the Company – can be worked out.

Preparation for the Transaction

We conduct a detailed financial analysis on behalf of the Company's board of directors outlining the parameters of a transaction that meet the goal above – reasonable for both the Company and the selling shareholder. Together with the Company's CFO, we make a comprehensive presentation to the Company's primary lender regarding financing for the potential leveraged share repurchase and are favorably received. Financing is available on reasonable terms through the company's regional bank.

The Company's attorney reviews the transaction and opines that there are no issues with state law and that the Company's board is duly authorized to engage in a transaction. The Company's CPA, in consultation with their national tax office, determines that there are no disadvantageous tax consequences to the Company and that the sale by the retiring owner is to be treated as a capital gains transaction.

Transaction Assumptions

Based on the above, the key assumptions of the leveraged share repurchase can now be summarized in Figure 13 on the next page.

The transaction is for the 30% block of shares being sold by the retiring owner. A decision has to be made regarding the use of cash on the Company's balance sheet, which would reduce the need for borrowing. Given the Company's ongoing profitability, ability to generate cash, and the availability of a line of credit, the decision is made to use all of the cash in the transaction.

The effective valuation multiple was 6.0x EBITDA. The board of directors requests that we formalize our initial calculations in the form of an appraisal for documentation of the transaction.

	Key Transaction Assumptions	Values	Comments
1	Number of Shares to be Purchased	300,000	30% of the outstanding shares
2	% of Cash Considered Excess	100.0%	Use all cash on balance sheet
3	EBITDA Multiple for Pricing Transaction	6.0	Assumption
4	Dollars of Current Annual Dividends	$3,000,000	Factual
5	Given Number of Shares for Example	100,000	10% block
6	Interest Rate on Pro Forma Cash	1.00%	Assumption per CFO
7	Interest Rate on Pro Forma Debt	6.00%	Assumption per bank discussions
8	Effective Tax Rate	36.20%	Factual
9	EBITDA Multiple for Pro Forma #1 Valuation	6.00	No Change in EBITDA multiple
10	Price/Earnings Multiple for Pro Forma #2	13.7	Proxy for future benefit of recap

Figure 13

The current dividend level is $3.0 million on an annual basis and the decision is made to leave the dividend intact at that level.

In a transaction, when cash is used, there is a loss of earnings on the former balance, so the pro forma financials recognize that there would be no interest earnings on the Company's prior cash balances. Similarly, the assumed rate on all debt, based on the discussions with the bank, is 6.0%. All pro forma debt is charged at this rate, so interest expense will increase by the amount of additional debt.

The Company's accountants determine that there should be no change in the blended federal and state income tax rate following the transaction, so the effective rate of 36.2% is used in our pro forma calculations.

We conduct a pro forma analysis, which values the business at the assumed multiple of 6.0x EBITDA.

Transaction Mechanics

The Company's equity was initially valued at $149 million. The 30% block is worth $44.8 million at that valuation, so we need to finance that amount. The financing is summarized in Figure 14.

Leveraged share re-purchases are a tool of corporate finance. Business owners who read this chapter should consider this concept for their own companies.

The $44.8 million purchase price is financed with $20.5 million of existing cash and $24.3 million of additional debt. In actuality, the existing debt of $16.4 million is refinanced, together with the new debt, providing for total long-term borrowings of $40.7 million, as indicated in Figure 14.

It is important to the bank and the Company's board of directors that there be a clear understanding of the impact of the transaction on the Company's balance sheet. We provide the summary balance sheet ratios as part of a more detailed analysis in Figure 15.

Where Figure 15 suggests that the pro forma results are reasonable, we made comparisons with the group of guideline public companies or with other industry metrics to reach those conclusions. The Company is reasonably capitalized following the transaction, meeting a concern of all parties.

We have examined the balance sheet, so now we need to see what impact the transaction has on the Company's income statement. Since this is a financial transaction, there is no impact on the Company's sales or normal operating expenses. Interest income and interest expense, however, will be impacted, as will earnings and the outstanding number of shares.

As seen at the bottom right of Figure 16, Pro Forma #1 indicates there is a 9.5% reduction in net income, which falls from $10.9 million actual to $9.9 million on a pro forma basis. The reduction in earnings is the result of the loss of interest income and increased interest expense, which is offset somewhat by the tax benefit of higher expenses and, therefore,

Contemplated Transaction

No. of Shares to be Purchased	Assumption #1	300,000	*30.0% of the shares*
Price Per Share		$149.41	
		$44,824,180	*Sets total amount for the repurchase*

Sources of Financing — Assumption #2

Internal Cash	100.0%	$20,484,662	*Cash to be used in repurchase*
Long-Term Borrowing for Transaction	Remainder	$24,339,518	
		$44,824,180	

Existing Debt Prior to Transaction	$16,409,839
Long-Term Borrowing for Transaction	$24,339,518
Pro Forma Debt	$40,749,357

Figure 14

Balance Sheet Ratios	Before	Pro Forma and Comments	
Current Ratio	4.4 *Lots of Liquidity*	3.5	Adequately liquid
Acid Test Ratio	2.2	1.3	Reasonable
Working Capital % of Sales	31.6%	23.5%	Reasonable
Total Liabilities / Assets	28.3%	47.5%	Reasonable
Total Liabilities / Equity	39.9%	91.8%	Reasonable
Interest Bearing Debt / Equity	13.0% *Low Leverage*	50.2%	Moderate leverage
Interest Bearing Debt / Assets	9.2%	26.0%	Reasonable
Assets / Equity	1.4	1.9	Reasonable
Debt / MVTC	11.3%	28.0%	Reasonable

Figure 15

lower income taxes. Note, however, at the bottom of Figure 16 that the number of shares outstanding is lowered from 1.0 million to 700 thousand, or some 30%. The difference in these two percentages, where the share reduction is greater than the lower earnings, lies at the heart of the financial engineering qualities of leveraged share repurchases.

There is no such thing as a free lunch. In paying for the shares in this leveraged repurchase, the Company's equity value is reduced dollar for dollar, unless that reduction is offset by favorable market perceptions of the repurchase. We see this reduction in Figure 17. The market value of equity falls from $149.4 million to $104.6 million, or 30%. That makes sense because the difference is the very same $44.8 million that is paid out in the transaction to the selling owner. With this sharp reduction in the market value of the Company's equity, what are the benefits?

Transaction Benefits

We are now in a position to see the benefits of a leveraged share repurchase for Acme Company and its shareholders. First, we know that the retiring shareholder is walking away with $44.8 million in gross proceeds that will be taxed at capital gains rates. The benefit to him of achieving total liquidity and the ability to diversify his wealth are readily apparent. What about the other promised benefits to the Company and to the remaining shareholders?

Benefits to the Company

As result of this leveraged share repurchase, Acme Company experiences a number of favorable benefits that are offset somewhat by the transactional impact on pro forma results. Two readily apparent benefits of the transaction are the enhancement in return on equity and enhancements achieved by a more optimal capital

Income Statement Analysis

	Actual	Adjustments	Pro Forma EBITDA Multiple Unchanged	% Change
Net Sales	$250,067,460		$250,067,460	
Cost of Sales	201,151,242		201,151,242	
Gross Profit	48,916,219		48,916,219	
Operating Expenses	31,011,600		31,011,600	
Operating Income/(Loss)	17,904,619		17,904,619	
Other Income/-Expense				
Interest Income / Pro Forma	297,903	(297,903)	0	
Interest Expense (-)	(1,118,574)	(1,326,387)	(2,444,961)	
Other, Net	0		0	
Total Other Income/-Expense	(820,671)		(2,444,961)	197.9%
Pre-Tax Income/(Loss)	17,083,947		15,459,657	-9.5%
Income Tax Expense/-Benefit	6,182,323	(585,927)	5,596,396	-9.5%
NET INCOME / (LOSS)	$10,901,625		$9,863,261	-9.5%
Shares Outstanding	1,000,000	(300,000)	700,000	-30.0%

Figure 16

Valuation Analysis

	Pre-Transaction		Pro Forma #1	% Change
	Assumption #3	Same Multiple	Assumption #9	
EBITDA	24,223,185		24,223,185	
Appropriate Multiple	6.0		6.0	0.0%
Market Value of Total Capital	145,339,111		145,339,111	0.0%
Less: Interest Bearing Debt	(16,409,839)	(24,339,518)	(40,749,357)	
Excess Cash	20,484,662	(20,484,662)	0	
Market Value of Equity	$149,413,933	($44,824,180)	$104,589,753	-30.0%

Figure 17

structure. Equity is being substituted for lower cost debt, which decreases the overall weighted average cost of capital (WACC), which reflects the portion of debt and equity present in the Company's capital structure. What this latter benefit means is that the shareholders can benefit from the transaction at a reasonable, or acceptable increase in risk.

Figure 18 (Returns) shows that while the net margin is reduced by 9.5% (from actual 4.4% to 3.9%), pro forma return on equity rises from 8.6% to 12.1%. In percentage terms, that's more than 40%. This leveraged share repurchase "engineers" an increase in return on equity from single digit levels to respectable double digits. The costs, in terms of leverage, are reasonable.

Note in Figure 18 that the transaction has no impact on EBITDA, which remains unchanged post-transaction. Assuming reasonable leverage, a leveraged share repurchase has no impact on the operations of the business. Excessive leverage, on the other hand, significantly increases risk and could potentially impair normal operations and the ability to generate sales and earnings.

Interest coverage (EBITDA/Interest Expense) is a healthy 9.9x post-transaction and the important measure of Debt/EBITDA remains conservative at 1.68x. Remember that the valuation multiple is 6.0x EBITDA, so there is substantial coverage here.

The company's Interest-Bearing Debt/Equity ratio rises from a nominal 13.0% to a reasonable 50.2%. We saw in Figure 15 above that the ratio of Debt/MVTC, which is the most relevant measure, is only 28% post-transaction. The "cost" of the transaction for Acme Company, in terms of increased leverage and risk, is acceptable. So there are clear benefits to Acme Company.

	Actual	Pro Forma #1	% Change
Returns			
Return on Equity	8.6%	12.1%	40.4%
EBITDA Margin	9.7%	9.7%	0.0%
Net Margin	4.4%	3.9%	-9.5%
Leverage			
EBITDA/Interest Expense	21.7	9.9	
Debt/EBITDA	0.68	1.68	
Interest-Bearing Debt/Equity	13.0%	50.2%	
Current Ratio	4.4	3.5	
EBITDA			
EBIT	17,904,619	17,904,619	0.0%
Depreciation & Amortization	6,318,566	6,318,566	0.0%
EBITDA (EBIT+depr)	$24,223,185	$24,223,185	0.0%

Figure 18

Benefits to Remaining Shareholders

We now turn to the important potential benefits of leveraged share repurchases for the remaining shareholders of the Company. If the owners of Acme Company are going to provide the retiring owner with $44.8 million in cash and no further risk associated with the Company, there need to be clear and compelling benefits to the remaining owners. This was an important consideration for the board of directors, of course.

The pro forma results of the leveraged share repurchase have the results or impacts for remaining owners as shown in Figure 19.

We already mentioned the reduction in shares outstanding. That is an important driver of the transaction results. Since the Company was valued at $149.41 per share ($149.4 million divided by 1.0 million shares), and since the selling shareholder was paid that same amount, the pro forma value for remaining shareholders is the same, or $149.41

per share. This assumes the Company is valued at 6.0x EBITDA and that the post-transaction price/earnings multiple falls from 13.7x to 10.6x. We finish this analysis with a look at what happens if there is any price/earnings multiple expansion as result of the transaction.

From the remaining shareholders' viewpoint, we make the following additional observations based on Figure 19:

- With 30% fewer shares outstanding and with pro forma net income falling only 9.5% (see above), earnings per share (EPS) increase from $10.90 to $14.09 per share (or 29.3%). That's a benefit worth thinking about.

- Given the assumption that the Company's dollar dividend will remain constant at $3.0 million, and that the dividend will be spread over 30% fewer shares, the dividend per share for remaining owners rises 42.9% to $4.29 per share (from $3.00 per share). Note that the pro forma dividend payout ratio

Shareholder Information	Actual		Pro-Forma #1	% Change
Shares Outstanding	1,000,000	(300,000)	700,000	-30.0%
Price Per Share	$149.41		$149.41	0.0%
Earnings Per Share	$10.90		$14.09	29.3%
Dividends per Share	$3.00		$4.29	42.9%
Book Value Per Share	$126.05		$116.04	-7.9%
Price/Earnings Multiple	13.7		10.6	
Price/Book Value	118.53%		128.76%	
Dividend Yield	2.008%		2.868%	
Dividend Payout Ratio	27.5%		30.4%	8.6%
Value of a Given Number of Remaining Shares	$14,941,393	100,000	$14,941,393	0.0%
Percentage of Company for Selected Block	10.0%	Assumption #5	14.3%	42.9%
Dividend Cash Flow for Those Same Shares	$300,000		$428,571	42.9%

Figure 19

remains reasonably conservative at 30.4%, reflecting only a modest increase from actual. The dividend payout ratio for the guideline public companies reflects a median of 44% by way of perspective.

- The dividend yield to remaining owners rises from 2.0% to 2.9%, which in itself is a significant increase in annual returns.

- Note that while the book value per share decreases modestly (-7.9%), the more important ratio of price/book value increased from 119% to 129%. There is more intangible asset value attributable to each post-transaction share than before.

- The highlighted box focuses on a 10% interest as representative of any interest in the Company. As with the value per share noted above, the post-transaction value of the assumed 100,000 share block remains the same, or $14.9 million. That, however, masks two key benefits of the transaction.

- The 100 thousand shares reflect a 10% ownership interest in the Company pre-transaction. After the transaction, the same 100,000 shares represent 14.3% of the equity ownership of the Company. This means that for every dollar of future increase in equity value, this remaining block will capture 14.3% of it, rather than 10.0%. This is a substantial benefit of the transaction.

- To put the impact on dividends in a more personal perspective, the initial 10% block received $300 thousand in annual dividends. Post-transaction, the same 100 thousand shares (14.3% of the total shares) will receive $429,000 in annual dividends.

It should be clear that the proposed leveraged share repurchase is favorable from the viewpoint of remaining owners. Their modestly increased financial risk of exposure to the Company is well offset by enhanced returns, increasing current dividend income, and a greater relative share in future appreciation.

Increased Focus on Shareholder Returns

An interesting thing about leveraged share repurchases like our example is that they do tend to focus management attention, not only on repaying debt, but also on continuing to achieve satisfactory returns for shareholders. They tend to keep management attention on maintaining a more optimal capital structure, as well.

There is a tendency among many closely held and family businesses to retire debt and accumulate excess assets when reinvestment opportunities are not attractive. There often is a reluctance to pay dividends for a variety of reasons. Most of these reasons are damaging to shareholder returns – even for the controlling owners who are reluctant to pay dividends. If the ownership of a company talks itself into a leveraged share repurchase, chances are that its management and owners will continue to be focused on achieving acceptable financial returns from the business following the transaction.

While management is focused on repaying debt, they also notice that the repayment of debt, absent significant reinvestment opportunities, tends to dampen future return on equity. This places attention on the potential for future leveraged share transactions or the implementation of a dividend policy to provide additional current returns to owners. With a combination of these policies, management and the board can engineer reasonable returns for investments in a business, even in a slow growth environment.

Conclusion

Talk about the concept of a leveraged share repurchase or a leveraged dividend recapitalization with your fellow owners and board of directors. Provide a copy of this book to your key advisers. Begin the conversation if it is appropriate for you. The timing is currently favorable:

- Valuations for most mainstream private companies are at reasonable levels such that transactions can occur that are beneficial for selling shareholders, companies and remaining owners.

- Interest rates remain at relatively low levels and lower interest costs enhance the benefits of leveraged share repurchases.

- Performance for many of our closely held clients is reasonable and their outlooks are decent in light of current economic forecasts.

- Many private companies have waited too long to engage in transactions of this nature and many aging owners need to sell out or to begin to diversify their holdings. They and their companies need to take action.

Leveraged share repurchases are a tool of corporate finance. Public companies and private equity firms use them extensively. The leveraged share repurchase tool is available to closely held and family business owners, as well. Business owners who read this chapter should consider this concept for their own companies.

CHAPTER 11

An ESOP as a Liquidity Alternative

What is an ESOP?

At the outset of this chapter, let me say that ESOPs have a certain amount of complexity attached. If you have no interest in the ESOP alternative or if you just hate complexity, skip to the next chapter.

An employee stock ownership plan (ESOP) is a "qualified," defined contribution employee benefit plan designed to invest primarily in the stock of the employing corporation (which establishes the ESOP Trust). When we use the term, ESOP, we are really talking about an ESOP Trust. The qualified aspect means tax-qualified if the ESOP and the sponsoring company follow rules established to protect the interests of employee beneficiaries of the ESOP.

Simplistically, the ESOP borrows money, which is guaranteed by the sponsoring corporation, to purchase stock of the company (the employer) from one or more selling shareholders. The ESOP then uses contributions from the company and/or distributions (S corporations and LLCs) or dividends (C corporations) to repay the debt.

Employees accrue benefits in shares of the company as the debt is repaid and the shares are released from a "suspense account," where unvested shares reside. Benefits accrue, like with qualified profit sharing plans, based on eligible compensation. When employees depart the company, they are entitled to receive their allocated (vested) shares, or their fair market value in cash and/or a promissory note.

Why Would You Use an ESOP for Liquidity?

If your company is similar to the kind of businesses described below, then you might want to consider an ESOP for partial (and, perhaps ultimately, total) liquidity for a number of reasons:

- **A properly structured ESOP can provide liquidity for a portion of an owner's shares at a reasonable price.** That reasonable price is "fair market value as determined by independent appraisal." This will not be a strategic price and will not reflect potential synergies. However, you might not receive that if you take your company to market, depending on the nature and position of your company within its industry.

- **You do not sell to outsiders.** You may have heard it said: "Nothing will change after the sale/merger." What you know is that things will change. When you sell to an ESOP, you typically have the same players doing the same things under a new ownership structure. If things change, it is because you and others want them to change.

- **Transparent financial management is necessary for the ESOP to succeed and for your employees to believe that it is a real benefit.** This is an important benefit, but it means that you and others in your company will have to communicate with your employees about the ESOP.

- **The ESOP may provide time for smooth, internal management transitions.**

- **Contributions and distributions to an ESOP are tax-deferred (and ultimately taxable to employee beneficiaries), so a dollar of cash flow received pro rata is a dollar available to pay principal and interest on the ESOP's debt.** This is a powerful benefit.

- **Because you didn't sell to outsiders, the benefit of ESOP debt pay-down is allocated to employees.** An ESOP in a successful company can generate substantial long-term benefits for employees.

- **An ESOP provides a very real benefit for employees, especially for S corporation ESOPs.** Distributions made by S corporations for the payment of taxes for other shareholders or otherwise flow into the ESOP on a tax-deferred basis. This benefit provides enhanced debt-service capabilities while there is leverage and enhanced cash flow to the ESOP when debt is retired.

When Do ESOPs Work Best?

Based on our experience in working with ESOPs for more than 30 years and with having an ESOP at Mercer Capital since 2006, ESOPs work best if the following conditions are met:

- Companies are consistently profitable and have stable and, preferably, growing earnings.

- Companies do not require heavy reinvestment in working capital, fixed assets or plant and equipment to grow. Service companies, professional service companies, distribution companies with decent margins, non-cyclical manufacturing business, and others may fit the bill.

- The owner(s) who desire(s) to sell have an interest in staying with the company for at least a period of years and a smooth management transition plan is in place for the future.

- The owner(s) desiring to sell do not desire to sell all of their stock so that the ESOP can establish and the company can learn about the ESOP absent the pressure of leverage for 100% of the stock. Note that ESOP transactions of whatever size are usually leveraged 100%. It is just easier for the parties to get comfortable with and prove the concept with smaller transactions at the outset.

ESOP Players

There are at least nine players in most ESOPs, or their functions must be filled if there are fewer. Let's go down the list and describe the functions:

1. **(Sponsoring) Company.** A company and its board of directors must sponsor the formation of an ESOP Trust to purchase shares of the company's stock.

2. **ESOP Trust (ESOP).** The trust is a fictitious person that is responsible for administering the plan in accordance with applicable rules and regulations.

3. **Trustee of the ESOP Trust.** The ESOP must have a trustee or trustees who accept a fiduciary liability that the ESOP will be run "for the sole benefit of the employee beneficiaries" and will be administered in accordance with applicable rules and regulations

4. **Selling Shareholder(s).** One or more shareholders must be willing to sell their shares to the ESOP based on a price determined by qualified independent appraisal (see below).

5. **Bank or Other Lender.** In most transactions, the Company will borrow money from a bank or other lender and will, in turn, lend the money to the ESOP (in a "mirror loan"). The ESOP uses the borrowings to purchase shares from selling shareholders.

6. **Employee Beneficiaries.** Generally, all full-time employees meeting certain hours of work and age requirements are eligible to participate in the ESOP.

7. **Plan Administrator.** Like with profit sharing plans, the details of administration are often performed by third party administrators who are hired by ESOP trustees.

8. **Business Appraiser.** Trustees are charged with purchasing shares for "not more than their fair market value." Trustees almost always retain the services of qualified business appraisers to provide independent appraisals as of the date of the ESOP transaction. The appraiser then provides an annual revaluation of the shares for plan administration purposes.

9. **Attorneys.** In most transactions, the sponsoring company will retain a qualified ESOP attorney, as will the trustee of the ESOP. In some instances, the selling shareholders will obtain their own counsel. In any transaction, there are any number of things that must be negotiated between the parties and, of course, every transaction must be fully documented.

Finally, sometimes companies will retain the services of an ESOP expert to "quarterback" the process and its many moving parts. These services normally reduce confusion and keep things moving on track and tend to reduce costs.

ESOP Transaction Mechanics

The diagram in Figure 20 serves as a visual guide to the mechanics of a leveraged ESOP transaction. Below the figure, we talk about the various transaction steps in the numbered items.

Let's assume that a company and a large shareholder have agreed that an ESOP will be a good vehicle to provide shareholder liquidity and shareholder benefits (more on that later). Further assume that the ESOP has been set up. We can now enter the diagram in Figure 20. Look first at the circle markers and follow the discussion by the numbers.

1a The company borrows funds to finance the stock purchase from a bank that approves the credit. The bank provides the funds to the company.

1b The company signs a note with the bank and agrees to guaranty the debt.

1c The selling shareholder in all likelihood will be required by the bank to sign a personal guaranty for the loan. If creditworthiness is an issue, the selling shareholder could be required to collateralize the guaranty with all or a portion of his net proceeds.

2a The company lends the funds it borrowed from the bank to the ESOP.

2b The ESOP, in turn, provides a note to the company that generally mirrors the terms of the company's loan with the bank.

3a The trustee retains the services of a qualified business appraiser who provides an independent opinion of the fair market value of the stock being transacted.

3b The trustee uses the appraisal as the basis for setting the price that the ESOP will pay for the shares.

4a The ESOP, using the funds borrowed from the company (in
& turn borrowed from the bank) purchases the stock from the
4b selling shareholder(s) and receives the stock certificates in return. At this point, the transaction is done. The bank holds the stock purchased by the ESOP as collateral in what is called a "suspense account."

Let's now switch to the square markers in Figure 20.

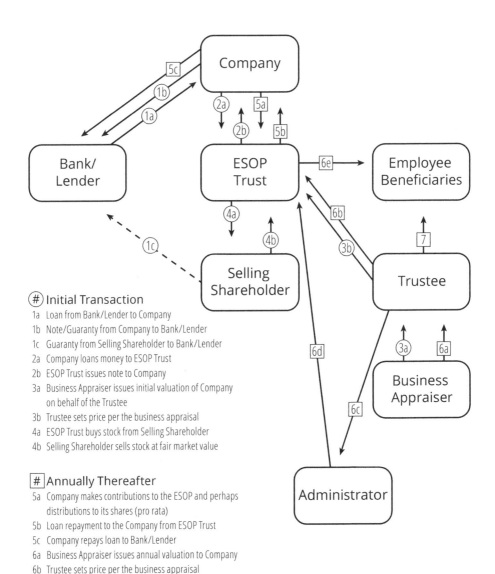

(#) Initial Transaction

1a Loan from Bank/Lender to Company
1b Note/Guaranty from Company to Bank/Lender
1c Guaranty from Selling Shareholder to Bank/Lender
2a Company loans money to ESOP Trust
2b ESOP Trust issues note to Company
3a Business Appraiser issues initial valuation of Company
    on behalf of the Trustee
3b Trustee sets price per the business appraisal
4a ESOP Trust buys stock from Selling Shareholder
4b Selling Shareholder sells stock at fair market value

Annually Thereafter

5a Company makes contributions to the ESOP and perhaps
    distributions to its shares (pro rata)
5b Loan repayment to the Company from ESOP Trust
5c Company repays loan to Bank/Lender
6a Business Appraiser issues annual valuation to Company
6b Trustee sets price per the business appraisal
6c Trustee provides appraisal and other information to
    the Administrator
6d Administrator prepares reporting and allocations
6e ESOP provides reporting to employees and distributes shares
    or cash to departing employees
7   Trustee has fiduciary responsibilities to Employee Beneficiaries

Figure 20

5a The company makes contributions to the ESOP based on eligible compensation. If dividends are paid (C corporations) or distributions occur (for taxes or otherwise for S corporations), the ESOP will share pro rata. Note that if S corporation distributions are made for pass-through taxes of non-ESOP shareholders, the ESOP will benefit pro rata, and will incur no present tax liability. This is pretty huge.

5b The ESOP will use both the contributions and any distributions to make interest and principal payments on its loan to the company. The bank will obviously want and/or perform an analysis to be sure that expected contributions plus distributions will appropriately amortize its debt. Shares are released from the suspense account to the ESOP based on principal reduction (there are complicated rules here), and the released shares are eligible for vesting with eligible employees.

5c The company, in turn, will take the funds repaid on its loan to the ESOP and make its interest and principal payments on its loan from the bank.

6a Each year-end, the trustee will retain the business appraiser to provide an independent opinion of the fair market value of the stock.

6b The trustee provides the appraised price for the ESOP as the basis for any transactions and/or allocations, and provides it to the Administrator.

6c The appraisal is used by the administrator as the basis for allocation and vesting of ESOP benefits.

6d The ESOP uses this information as the basis for transactions that occur.

6e The administrator's reports are provided to employees at the instruction of the ESOP trustee.

7 The administrator's report is the basis for transactions that occur as described in #6 above.

As with all qualified retirement plans, there are rules and requirements pertaining to annual contribution limits, vesting, share allocation, plan administration, and other functional aspects that are beyond the scope of this chapter.

Personal Experience with an ESOP

I can't tell you that you should consider an ESOP as a means of obtaining partial liquidity for your shares in your company. But I can tell you that, after considering all of the information above, and more, since I've been working with ESOPs for 30-plus years, we installed an ESOP at Mercer Capital effective January 1, 2006.

The ESOP purchased 49.9% of the shares from me and our then-president, who is now retired. Like in the chart and discussion above, we had all the players:

1. Mercer Capital retained the services of an experienced attorney who has formed many ESOPs to perform the role of "quarterback" for our transaction.

2. The Company formed an ESOP Trust.

3. We retained the services of an independent trustee to represent the ESOP's and employees' interests in the transaction.

4. The ESOP trustee retained the services of a qualified business appraiser, who provided the needed determination of fair market value, but also reviewed the transaction and provided a fairness opinion from the viewpoint of the ESOP and its beneficiaries. The trustee also retained a law firm experienced in similar transactions.

5. Mercer Capital also retained separate legal counsel for purposes of the transaction.

6. Mercer Capital borrowed funds from our bank and guaranteed the loan, signing a corporate promissory note. The bank retained counsel to review the documents from its viewpoint (at Mercer Capital's expense).

7. Mercer Capital then made a "mirror loan" to the ESOP in exchange for its promissory note.

8. The other shareholder and I each had to guaranty our respective portions of the loan personally.

9. The ESOP used the cash from the loan to purchase shares from me and the other shareholder.

10. The ESOP is now trusteed by two senior employees who have access to an independent trustee when and if needed. The trustees retained the services of an administration firm and have continued to retain the original appraiser to provide the annual reappraisals for administration purposes.

An ESOP provides a very real benefit for employees, especially for S corporation ESOPs.

We used a quarterback and worked to prevent disagreements while the deal was being negotiated. We held costs to a reasonable level. Your results may vary, even significantly.

It is now eight years later. The ESOP has repaid its totally leveraged loan to Mercer Capital in its entirety and Mercer Capital has repaid its loan to our bank. This means that all of the shares that were purchased by the ESOP in 2006 have been allocated to current (and a few former) employees.

Our employees are beneficiaries of substantial value represented by the 49.9% of Mercer Capital's stock owned by the ESOP. In addition, the ESOP, and the employees through it, receives 49.9% of the distributable earnings of our company in the form of allowable contributions and distributions to shareholders on a going forward basis. This stream of cash flow will be used by the ESOP trustees to purchase shares from departed employees, and perhaps from me, as well. Over time, the ESOP should also be able to invest in assets other than Mercer Capital stock for the benefit of the ESOP's employee beneficiaries.

Should You Consider an ESOP?

Should you consider an ESOP to obtain partial liquidity from your investment in your closely held or family business? We cannot answer that question for you. Sellers of stock to an ESOP may enjoy certain tax benefits related to their sale proceeds, and the Company (the sponsor) may enjoy tax benefits related to its contributions to the ESOP so an ESOP can be a tax-advantaged exit strategy.

ESOPs are somewhat complex. Under the right circumstances, an ESOP can provide an excellent ownership and management transitioning vehicle. If you think this liquidity option fits your situation, know that some 10,000 other ESOP companies in the United States have been able to figure it out. You can as well.

CHAPTER 12

Minority Interest Private Equity Investments

Many business owners believe that the only way to access the private equity markets is to sell all of their companies to private equity (PE) funds. This belief is increasingly becoming outdated. A growing number of PE funds currently invest primarily in minority (i.e., non-control) situations.

Private Equity Minority Investments on the Upswing

During 2013, about 40% of all PE investments involved less than control transactions. Competition for deals and $1 trillion of available "dry powder" is causing an increasing number of PE funds to consider less than control investments.

The time may be ripe for closely held and family business owners to consider the option of private equity when liquidity and/or growth capital are desired while maintaining control of a business.

Recent statistics indicate that 15% of companies with enterprise values greater than $500 million are owned by private equity funds. Alternatively, only 3% of firms with enterprise values of less than $100 million are owned by PE funds. With so much investment capacity in the PE world searching for deals, now may be time to consider taking on a PE partner to provide liquidity for aging owners and/or to obtain growth capital to accelerate growth opportunities.

PE firms are increasingly looking for successful closely held and family businesses in which to invest because often they cannot find sufficient transaction volume in change of control transactions.

Is Private Equity a Reasonable Alternative?

A number of closely held and family businesses feel the need to access outside capital for liquidity and diversification purposes, as well as for growth capital. However, the PE world has had a somewhat ruthless reputation. There is always the fear that the legacy of the company and the owners will be trashed and that the business will end up on the chopping block.

In the current market environment, significant capital can often be obtained from PE investors who will buy less of a business, say 30% to 49%, and exert less than full control.

In the current market environment, significant capital can often be obtained from PE investors who will buy less of a business, say 30% to 49%, and exert less than full control. An advantage of working with minority investors is that a company's owner(s) can sell significant portions of their equity, thereby achieving partial liquidity and diversification opportunities and have a second bite at the apple down the road.

We recently worked with a company that sold 49% of its equity to a private equity firm with its founder achieving substantial liquidity while retaining control. There were, of course, covenants that the company had to maintain along the way and certain personnel changes required concurrence from the minority investor. Nevertheless, the founder retained substantial control of the business.

After a few years, there was agreement between the founder and the minority investor to sell the company to a strategic acquirer at a phenomenal price. It was a good investment for the PE firm and a great two-step road to liquidity for the founder.

Three Reasons to Consider Private Equity

There are at least three reasons for a successful closely held or family business to consider engaging in a minority interest transaction with a private equity firm.

1. **Satisfy liquidity/diversification needs while retaining a significant share in a favorable upside outlook.** This was the case for the company mentioned above. Owners may not want to lose control when they see a significant upside. Minority investors can provide the equity for needed liquidity while allowing owners to stay involved and to share in the upside.

2. **Capital and expertise are required to access available opportunities.** Many private companies face significant domestic or international expansion opportunities. Accessing those opportunities may require capital expenditures and be facilitated by minority investors with relevant expertise. Transactions to facilitate such opportunities can also be structured to provide liquidity for selling owners.

3. **Outside counsel needed to take the business to the next level.** Some private companies achieve ceilings on their growth. The companies are sound, but additional experience is needed at the board and strategic levels to enable them to penetrate their ceilings.

Things Won't Be Quite the Same After the Deal

As stated numerous times before, there is no such thing as a free lunch. If you sell a minority stake in your business to a private equity firm, things will be different following the transaction. While the minority investors will not have control, they will negotiate certain elements of control before they will make an investment. Think about the following before engaging in a transaction to increase the potential for having a good working relationship with your new investor(s).

- **The private equity time line.** If you sell a portion of your business to a PE investor, you are renting the capital. The typical PE investor wants liquidity within five to seven years and expects a return of 15% to 20% (or more if they can buy cheaply enough). After that time, they will want to sell the company to achieve liquidity or, in the alternative, they will want you and your fellow owners to buy them out. You have to be sure that your time line will reasonably match your minority investor's time line.

- **Private equity covenants (agreements).** The stock purchase agreement with a PE minority investor will almost certainly contain covenants that provide elements of control to them when certain things happen (or don't happen). For example, there may be a covenant calling for a minimum EBITDA level. If the company performs below this level, certain elements of control may be ceded to the PE investors. There may also be capital expenditure approvals in the event that you desire expenditures above certain agreed upon levels.

- **Key personnel changes.** Your PE investor may desire the right to approve certain key personnel changes. They buy into your company with one set of expectations and want to be on board if you want to change the game on them.

Private equity investors have a great deal of capital looking to be placed with good companies. Don't forget, however, that while every investor's money is green, if you take on a significant minority investor, you need to get comfortable with them to assure the greatest probability for a successful working relationship during your time together. This means that while your PE investors are doing their due diligence about your company, you will need to be doing your due diligence about them. Talk to other owners in companies where they have invested. Spend enough time dating to be sure that you have time to get comfortable.

Sources for statistics from this chapter:

- Michelle Park Lazette, "Who's in control? Private equity firms don't have to be," Cleveland Business, August 27, 2013.

- Dan Primack, "Private equity 'overhang' tops $1 trillion," www. fortune.com, March 5, 2014 (citing Bain & Company's private equity reports).

- Mary Josephs, "Four Reasons Middle Market Companies Shouldn't Wait for Private Equity," www.forbes.com, March 5, 2014 (citing study by Bain & Company).

Business owners who take the advice in this book seriously will take time to consider liquidity and diversification options like taking on a private equity investor. This option may be the farthest thing from your mind, but it is one worthy of consideration.

CHAPTER 13

Buy-Sell Agreements and Life Insurance

Buy-sell agreements are ownership transition plans in disguise. Few business owners think about their buy-sell agreements in this light, but if your agreement is triggered, either through the death of a shareholder or otherwise, then ownership will change hands.

In this chapter, we briefly discuss the primary types of buy-sell agreements and ask you to think about your own agreements in light of this brief introduction to the topic. I've written on buy-sell agreements extensively, and point you to that literature for further study.

Also discussed is the relationship between life insurance and buy-sell agreements. Life insurance proceeds can be used as a funding vehicle to repurchase shares of a deceased owner. In such cases, the pro-

Your buy-sell agreement is really ownership transition on autopilot. The real question is whether you, the other owners and the company will land safely when a trigger event occurs or if some or all of you will crash and burn.

ceeds are not part of value. However, life insurance proceeds can also be considered as a corporate asset, in which case the proceeds are added to value in the determination of the price at which transactions occur.

The differences between these two treatments can be significant, and business owners need to be sure they understand and decide and document how life insurance proceeds will be treated when buy-sell agreements are triggered. If the documents are not clear, then bad things can occur.

Finally, while looking at the insurance question, we will point out that the operation of buy-sell agreements can create intended and perhaps unintended consequences in the ownership structure of companies. In reading this chapter, please keep these three questions in mind:

1. Do you know what will happen if your buy-sell agreement is triggered?

2. Do you know how your buy-sell agreement and related documents call for treatment of any life insurance proceeds upon the death of an owner?

3. Do you know what will happen to ownership of your business if your buy-sell agreement is triggered?

Types of Buy-Sell Agreements

There are three basic types of buy-sell agreements. They are fixed price agreements, formula agreements, and agreements where one or more appraisers are used to establish the price for buy-sell agreement purposes.

Fixed Price Buy-Sell Agreements

With fixed price agreements, the owners of a company must agree on a price for their buy-sell agreement at a point in time and then, must have a regular process for re-agreeing on the price over time. It is often easy to agree on a price the first time a price is set. Perhaps there has been a transaction, or maybe the owners have just invested. So agreement is reached.

The problem comes with the passage of time. Value changes, either up or down, and the circumstances of the owners may also change.

If your buy-sell agreement has a fixed price method for determining transaction prices following trigger events, it is a good idea to know what that price will be and how it is set and reset. Most fixed price buy-sell agreements are set at a point in time and then are not reset on a regular basis. As a result, the fixed prices in many buy-sell agreements may bear little relationship to the reasonable market values (or fair market values) of many companies today.

If the price is higher than current value and you are a remaining buyer, you will overpay, perhaps significantly, for the shares of a deceased owner. The estate will get a very favorable price at the expense of you, any other shareholders, and the company.

If the price is lower than current value and you are triggered, you or your estate will suffer from a low price while the other owners and the company will benefit.

Neither possibility is what you would agree to if the owners all sat down today to set a price.

Your fixed price buy-sell agreement may be a ticking time bomb.

Needless to say, I don't recommend the use of fixed price agreements for obvious reasons.

Formula Buy-Sell Agreements

Many business owners want a (simple) formula for setting the price at which transactions will occur after their buy-sell agreements are triggered.

Formula buy-sell agreements use a formula or formulas to establish the price for purposes of buy-sell agreements. The problems with formulas are numerous, and no formula I've seen to date can set the price for a company over time given changes in the economy, financing conditions, industry conditions, and in the company itself.

If your buy-sell agreement has a formula pricing mechanism, has anyone calculated the formula recently? What is the result? Is it reasonable? If so, how do you know?

If your agreement has a formula and no one has calculated it, then you don't know the answers to the previous questions.

If your buy-sell agreement has a formula, is there any basis for making adjustments to it if certain unusual things happen? Disastrous results can occur when a formula does not allow for even obvious adjustments for non-recurring or unusual items, either positive or negative, that should have minimal impact on value, but which can have enormous impact absent adjustments.

And if adjustments are needed, who will decide on what the appropriate or necessary adjustments should be? The parties have adverse interests when an agreement is triggered.

Your formula buy-sell agreement may be a ticking time bomb.

Multiple Appraiser Buy-Sell Agreements

Buy-sell agreements calling for appraisers come in two types, those calling for two or more appraisers to work through an appraisal process to reach the price, and those calling for a single appraiser to prepare an appraisal to set the price.

Let's begin with multiple appraiser processes. Many buy-sell agreements have pricing mechanisms that call for the selling party to select an appraiser and for the buying party (usually the company) to select another appraiser. These two appraisers then prepare appraisals. If their conclusions are within (almost always) 10% of each other, the price will be the average. But the conclusions are almost always more than 10% apart.

If there is a large difference, the two original appraisers will select a third appraiser who is supposed to save the day. His conclusion may be averaged with the other two, or averaged with the closer of the other two, or it may be conclusive of value.

The point is, no one knows what the conclusion will be until the end of a long, expensive and divisive process. Quite often there is litigation involved. Quite often there is disagreement over qualifications of appraisers, or differences in the background and experience of the appraisers selected that create yet other issues.

My point is that if you have a multiple appraiser buy-sell agreement, you really don't know with any degree of certainty what will happen if a trigger event occurs.

Your multiple appraiser buy-sell agreement may be a ticking time bomb.

Single Appraiser Buy-Sell Agreements

I have long recommended that the preferred pricing mechanism for the buy-sell agreements of most successful private business has the following elements:

- **A single appraiser is agreed upon by the parties.** All agree on background, experience and credentials of the appraiser and the firm. The appraiser is named in the buy-sell agreement to memorialize the agreement of the parties. The appraiser is retained by the company on behalf of all parties to the buy-sell agreement.

- **The selected appraiser provides a draft valuation to all parties.** The parties review the draft and all have the opportunity to see exactly what kind of value the appraiser develops. There is then a chance for revision and additional negotiation. The appraiser treats life insurance as agreed to by the parties. When all have had input to the appraiser, the appraisal is finalized. This appraisal conclusion becomes the price for the buy-sell agreement.

- **Next year (or within two years at most) the appraiser provides a revaluation.** This revaluation resets the price for the buy-sell agreement until the next reappraisal.

- **If there is a trigger event, the selected appraiser provides a revaluation.** The agreement may call for the existing price if the trigger event is within an agreed upon number of months of the last appraisal. In any event, the process is known in advance. The parties have already agreed on the appraiser. The appraiser will provide the reappraisal as of the trigger event and reconcile his conclusion with the prior appraisal based on what has happened with the company and other external factors. There is little room for disagreement.

This single appraiser process solves virtually all of the problems outlined above with the other appraisal mechanisms.

If you don't know what will happen when your buy-sell agreement is triggered, get with your fellow owners and advisers to revise your agreement in line with the single appraiser process recommendation just outlined. Further resources discussing this concept can be found here:

- *Buy-Sell Agreements for Closely Held and Family Business Owners* (Print book available at www.ChrisMercer.net/books/ and www.MercerCapital.com)

- *Buy-Sell Agreements for Baby Boomer Business Owners* (Amazon Kindle book)

Life Insurance Associated with Buy-Sell Agreements

If there is life insurance associated with your buy-sell agreement, it is critical to be sure that the language in the agreement and any related documents specifies its treatment precisely. Life insurance can be used as a funding vehicle to acquire the stock of a deceased owner. If so, the life insurance proceeds are not treated as part of the purchase price. Alternatively, life insurance can be a corporate asset (corporate-owned life insurance, or COLI), and proceeds are part of value.

The two different treatments provide different, perhaps dramatically different results for selling owners and remaining owners when buy-sell agreements are triggered by the death of an owner.

The following discussion provides an overview of the differences in treatment of life insurance on the financial condition of the company and of the shareholders, both deceased and remaining, as well as their ownership positions. We will show two hypothetical examples:

- Harry and Charles own a company, with each owning 50% of the stock. There is adequate life insurance in place, and Harry dies.

- Harry, Charles and William own a company, with each owning 40%, 30%, and 30%, respectively. William dies.

We look at each of these hypotheticals under two assumptions regarding life insurance treatment:

- **Funding Vehicle.** The life insurance proceeds are intended to be a funding vehicle to repurchase the shares of a deceased owner. In this case, life insurance proceeds are not included in value to determine the price for buy-sell agreement transactions.

- **Corporate Asset.** The life insurance is intended to be a corporate asset. The proceeds are, therefore, included in value to determine the price for buy-sell agreement transactions.

The distinction between the two hypotheticals creates a difference in equity value equivalent to the life insurance proceeds received by a company upon the death of a shareholder. It is that difference that makes it vitally important for business owners to pay careful attention to the link between buy-sell agreements and the use of life insurance proceeds upon the death of an insured shareholder.

Two Equal Owners: Examples 1a and 1b

Harry and Charles own the company equally. The company is worth $10 million, which has been established by the single appraiser agreed to in the buy-sell agreement. The agreement is assumed, for Example 1a, to call for the life insurance proceeds to be used as a funding vehicle, so *the proceeds are not included in value* for purposes of the buy-sell agreement.

We see on Lines 2 and 3 in Figure 21 that Harry and Charles own 50% of the company each and their ownership interests are valued at $5 million each based on the appraisal, which does not consider life insurance in the valuation. The company has life insurance policies of $6 million each on the lives of Harry and Charles. Unfortunately, Harry died. Shortly thereafter, life insurance proceeds of $6 million were received by the company.

The proceeds are considered for the company (Line 6 of Figure 21) and Harry's estate is paid the $5 million it is owed per the buy-sell agreement (Lines 9 and 10 of Figure 21). Harry's shares are retired.

Charles now owns 100% of the 50 shares remaining outstanding, and the company is worth $11 million, since there was $1 million of over-insurance on Harry's life. As result of the operation of the buy-sell agreement, Charles' interest increased more than $6 million in value (i.e., more than 100%) as result of the operation of the buy-sell agreement.

Harry's estate received $5 million, which was 50% of the pre-death value of the company. One can argue that this arrangement is not fair to Harry's estate, because of the disproportionate shift in value towards

Example 1a: Life Insurance is Funding Vehicle

		Company	Estate Harry	Charles
1	Stock Ownership (Shares)	100	50	50
2	Stock Ownership (%)	100%	50%	50%
3	Pre-Life Insurance Value ($000)	$10,000	$5,000	$5,000
4	Life Insurance Coverage		120%	120%
5	Life Insurance		$6,000	$6,000
6	Life Insurance Proceeds	$6,000		
7	Repurchase Liability	($5,000)		
8	Post-Life Insurance Value	$11,000		
9	Repurchase Stock ($)	($5,000)	$5,000	
10	Retire / Sell Stock	(50)	(50)	0
11	Remaining Shares	50	0	50
12	New Stock Ownership (%)	100.0%	0.0%	100.0%
13	Post-Life Insurance Value of Co.	$11,000	$0	$11,000
14	Post Life Insurance Value		$5,000	$11,000
15	Net Change in Value from Repurchase	$1,000	$0	$6,000

Figure 21

Charles. However, the result would have been the same but in Harry's favor had Charles been the first to die.

Now we look at Example 1b in Figure 22 in which the appraiser is instructed to consider the life insurance as a corporate asset and therefore *the proceeds are included in value* for purposes of the buy-sell agreement.

At Line 7 of Figure 22, we see that the appraised value, including the life insurance proceeds, is $16 million, and Harry's estate value is $8 million (as is Charles' value). This means that the repurchase liability is $8 million, or $2 million greater than the life insurance proceeds of $6 million.

Example 1b: Life Insurance is a Corporate Asset

		Company	Estate Harry	Charles
1	Stock Ownership (Shares)	100	50	50
2	Stock Ownership (%)	100%	50%	50%
3	Pre-Life Insurance Value ($000)	$10,000	$5,000	$5,000
4	Life Insurance Coverage		120%	120%
5	Life Insurance		$6,000	$6,000
6	Life Insurance Proceeds/Allocation	$6,000	$3,000	$3,000
7	Post Life Insurance Value	$16,000	$8,000	$8,000
8	Repurchase Liability	($8,000)		
9	Post-Life Insurance Value	$8,000		

		Company	Estate Harry	Charles
10	Repurchase Stock ($)	($8,000)	$8,000	
11	Retire / Sell Stock	(50)	(50)	0
12	Remaining Shares	50	0	50
13	New Stock Ownership (%)	100.0%	0.0%	100.0%
14	Post-Life Insurance Value of Co.	$8,000	$0	$8,000
15	Post Life Insurance Value		$8,000	$8,000
16	Net Change in Value from Repurchase	($2,000)	$3,000	$3,000

Figure 22

The shares are redeemed (Lines 10 and 11 of Figure 22), with the company borrowing $2 million to accomplish the purchase. The company's equity value is reduced by the extent of the payment in excess of the life insurance proceeds.

Harry's estate received $8 million, or $3 million more than the value prior to the consideration of life insurance. Charles owns 100% of a company now worth $8 million with $2 million of leverage that did not previously exist.

We make no value judgments regarding these two treatments. However, I suggest that if you have life insurance in connection with a buy-sell agreement, differences of this magnitude call for the parties to discuss and to understand what they are agreeing to in the negotiation. The results are significantly different for both Harry and Charles under Example 1a and Example 1b.

If the documentation linking life insurance to the buy-sell purchase is not clear, the estate of a selling shareholder under similar conditions as this example will likely argue that the life insurance was intended to be a corporate asset. The estate is selling and desires the highest possible price. Naturally, the company would likely desire that the insurance be treated as a funding vehicle, and the selling shareholder (the estate) would likely desire that it be treated as an asset of the company. Litigation can result.

I testified in a case with facts similar to the examples above. However, the appraiser was not given instruction regarding life insurance treatment. The appraiser determined that it was "fair" to treat the proceeds as a corporate asset. The company disagreed with the appraiser and there was litigation. Ultimately the court agreed with the appraiser based on certain language in the buy sell agreement.

Three Large Owners: Example 2a and 2b

In the second hypothetical example, we have three owners, Harry Charles and William. Harry owns the largest share (40%), and Charles and William own 30% each. No one owner is in control of the business, so at least two owners must agree on significant decisions, and any two owners can jointly exert control.

Example 2a in Figure 23 assumes that life insurance is a funding vehicle and *the proceeds are not included in value* for purposes of the buy-sell agreement.

In this example, William, a 30% owner died. William's share of value excluding life insurance proceeds is $3 million and the life insurance on his life is $3.6 million (Lines 5 and 6 of Figure 23). The company redeems his shares (Lines 9 and 10), and there are 70 shares remaining

Example 2a: Life Insurance is Funding Vehicle

	Company	Harry	Charles	Estate William
1	Stock Ownership (Shares)	100	40	30	30
2	Stock Ownership (%)	100%	40%	30%	30%
3	Pre-Life Insurance Value ($000)	$10,000	$4,000	$3,000	$3,000
4	Life Insurance Coverage		120%	120%	120%
5	Life Insurance Allocation		$4,800	$3,600	$3,600
6	Life Insurance Proceeds	$3,600			
7	Repurchase Liability	($3,000)			
8	Post-Life Insurance Value	$10,600			
9	Repurchase Stock ($)	($3,000)			$3,000
10	Retire / Sell Stock	(30)	0	0	(30)
11	Remaining Shares	70	40	30	0
12	New Stock Ownership (%)	100.0%	57.1%	42.9%	0.0%
13	Post-Life Insurance Value of Co.	$10,600	$6,057	$4,543	$0
14	Post Life Insurance Value			$4,543	$3,000
15	Net Change in Value from Repurchase	$600	$2,057	$1,543	$0

Figure 23

outstanding (Line 11). Note on (Line 12) that Harry's share of ownership increased from 40% to 57.1%, so the operation of the buy-sell agreement left him with legal control of the business.

This may have been an intended or unintended consequence, but it definitely changes the working relationship between Harry and Charles relative to the non-control situation that existed prior to William's death.

As in Example 1a in Figure 21, William's estate received the pro rata
share of pre-insurance value, or $3 million. We've already noted the
change of control. Now look at the post-life insurance values for Harry

Example 2b: Life Insurance is a Corporate Asset

		Company	Harry	Charles	Estate William
1	Stock Ownership (Shares)	100	40	30	30
2	Stock Ownership (%)	100%	40%	30%	30%
3	Pre-Life Insurance Value ($000)	$10,000	$4,000	$3,000	$3,000
4	Life Insurance Coverage		120%	120%	120%
5	Life Insurance		$4,800	$3,600	$3,600
6	Life Insurance Proceeds/Allocation	$3,600	$1,440	$1,080	$1,080
7	Post Life Insurance Value	$13,600	$5,440	$4,080	$4,080
8	Repurchase Liability	($4,080)			
9	Post-Life Insurance Value	$9,520			
10	Repurchase Stock ($)	($4,080)			$4,080
11	Retire / Sell Stock	(30)	0	0	(30)
12	Remaining Shares	70	40	30	0
13	New Stock Ownership (%)	100.0%	57.1%	42.9%	0.0%
14	Post-Life Insurance Value of Co.	$9,520	$5,440	$4,080	$0
15	Post Life Insurance Value				$4,080
16	Net Change in Value from Repurchase	($480)	$1,440	$1,080	$1,080

Figure 24

and Charles, which increase more than 50% each relative to pre-transaction (Lines 13 and 15 of Figure 24). Harry's value rises from $4 million to $6.1 million, and Charles has a similar increase, rising from $3 million to $4.5 million.

In Example 2b in Figure 24, life insurance is considered to be a corporate asset and the life insurance *proceeds are included in value* for purposes of the buy-sell agreement.

In Example 2b, William is still the owner who died. Life insurance proceeds of $3.6 million are received by the company (Line 6), which would seem to be sufficient to pay the $3 million of value found for William's estate on Line 3 of Figure 24. However, the life insurance is added to value in this example.

William's estate shares in 30% of the $3.6 million of life insurance proceeds, so the estate is owed $4.1 million for its shares. As a result, the company must borrow $480 thousand in addition to the life insurance proceeds of $3.6 million in order to purchase William's shares from his estate for $4.1 million (Line 10 of Figure 24).

In Example 2b of Figure 24, both Harry and Charles receive their pro rata share of the increased value attributable to the life insurance proceeds, so their values increase some 36% (as did William's shares).

As in Example 2a of Figure 23, the operation of the buy-sell agreement shifted control of the business to Harry.

There is another alternative that we did not show. Had Harry died owning 40% of the company, Charles and William would have equal 50% ownership interests. In that event, no one would have control and the ownership dynamic would be different still. The other results would have been numerically different but conceptually the same.

Concluding Thoughts on the Different Treatments

We have not covered all possible ownership situations, or all possible life insurance situations. However, the examples above provide insight into the differences that the two treatments for life insurance proceeds can have on the parties to buy-sell agreements.

After thinking about the potential impacts of the different treatments of life insurance, we put together a preliminary, qualitative analysis of certain positive and negative or potentially negative aspects for consideration.

Readers can draw their own conclusions. We make no value judgments

	Company	Remaining Owners	Deceased Owner
Funding Vehicle	+ Clean purchase of deceased owner's shares + Minimizes impact of repurchase on company + Potential increase in value − Cost of insurance must be borne	+ Receive pickup in value + Receive pickup in ownership + Compensation for incurring cost of life insurance − Cost of insurance must be borne	+ There is ready funding vehicle for repurchase + Estate gains full liquidity − Cost of insurance must be borne − No sharing in pickup value or ownership − No compensation for bearing cost of insurance
Corporate Asset	+ Proceeds increase value − Cost of insurance must be borne − Increases impact of repurchase on company	+ Pickup in value, but shared with deceased + Pickup in ownership + Compensation for incurring cost of life insurance − Cost of insurance must be borne	+ There is ready funding vehicle for repurchase + Estate gains full liquidity + Pickup in value from life insurance proceeds + Compensation for incurring life of insurance

Figure 25

about the differences in treatment in either Example 1 (a and b) or Example 2 (a and b). However, we do suggest that owners of companies with buy-sell agreements and associated life insurance companies should make themselves aware of the potential effects on ownership transfer and wealth transfer that might occur if the agreements are triggered.

Looking at Figure 25, there is a certain rationale, particularly when life insurance is considered as a funding vehicle and not included in value, for instructing the appraiser to normalize earnings in the valuation process for the cost of life insurance. That suggestion might be to normalize for the cost of the deceased owner's policy. However, the logic could as well call for normalization of the cost of all policies supporting the buy-sell agreement.

Concluding Observations about Buy-Sell Agreements

We conclude this chapter by making several observations for your consideration.

- It matters how the price is set for purposes of your buy sell agreement. We talked above about problems with fixed price and formula agreements. And the issues with multiple appraiser agreements are numerous as well.

- I have long recommended that a single appraiser process is the preferred pricing mechanism for most buy-sell agreements. If you want further resources, you can try the books at the end of the chapter or go to my blog (www.ChrisMercer.net) to find additional resources to help you with your buy-sell agreements.

- I am not an attorney, so anything I say about buy-sell agreements is from business and valuation perspectives only. Your attorney needs to be involved with your review, as do, perhaps, your financial adviser and your accountant. And certainly, a qualified business appraiser should be involved, as well.

- Life insurance is often used to fund the payment of stock repurchases under buy-sell agreements. It matters greatly how the agreements are written. By the agreements, I mean the buy-sell agreement and any documentation pertaining to the related life insurance.

- Life insurance needs to be reviewed regularly along with buy-sell agreements. I am not a life insurance specialist, but your life insurance consultant should also be involved as you review your life insurance and your buy-sell agreement.

- Ownership transition and management transition require team-work if they are to work effectively. The transitions potentially created by the operation of your buy-sell agreement are simply too important to ignore.

Resources Available

1. *Buy Sell Agreements for Closely Held and Family Business Owners* (print book, $25.00 plus shipping and handling – available at www.ChrisMercer.net and www.MercerCapital.com)

2. *Buy Sell Agreements for Baby Boomer Business Owners* (Amazon Kindle Book). Link through www.ChrisMercer.net or go directly to Amazon.com, currently priced at $2.99 to encourage you to download.

3. Buy Sell Agreement Review Checklist (available at www.ChrisMercer.net and www.MercerCapital.com)

4. Checklist for Shareholder Promissory Notes (available at www.ChrisMercer.net and www.MercerCapital.com)

5. My blog, www.ChrisMercer.net/blog, contains additional posts and information about b 🔑 agreements.

Buy-sell agreements cry out for periodic review. These agreements are extremely important for ownership transition. They too often operate on autopilot and no one knows what will happen. Will your autopilot buy-sell agreement provide a safe landing, or will you, your company and your other owners crash and burn if it is triggered?

Perspectives on Managing Private Company Wealth

CHAPTER 14

What is Transferable Business Value?

Consider that there are two kinds of value for your business.

1. Value to you as an owner

2. Transferable value

These concepts are fairly simple and straightforward, but they are nevertheless important to understand as we talk about successful ownership and management transitions.

Value to You as an Owner

Ownership of a business, or of a significant portion of a business, especially when that ownership conveys the right to work in the business, can have special value.

There is a concept known as *investment value*. Investment value relates to value from the perspective of a particular owner. Any given business may not be worth the same to every potential owner. And the value of a business may have unique value to a particular owner, for example, the current one, for a number of reasons, including:

- **The business represents life.** The business owner is so devoted to the business that he cannot imagine life without owning and working at the business. In my more than 30 years in the business valuation profession, I have seen numerous clients and other business owners who never left their businesses – until the moment they died. I've seen numerous others who missed good, great, or even phenomenal opportunities to transition their businesses because they could not let go.

- **The business represents position and prestige.** Some business owners get caught up in their positions in their companies, their communities, and their industries – all of which they believe are the result of their owning and working at a successful business. This makes it difficult to step down. There may be similarities between this and the first reason, but their psychological under-pinnings are different.

- **The business represents lifestyle.** Particularly with some smaller businesses, but even in businesses of significant size and value, the owners' incomes and benefits may provide a larger lifestyle than is available from investment income from the value of the business. This can be a real trap. Before successful transitions can occur, this problem must be resolved, either by an increase in the value of the business, or by a reduction in life-style, or a combination of the two.

- **The owner is a key person.** The owner may be extremely critical to the ongoing success of the business, either because of spe-cial knowledge or expertise, customer or supplier relationships, unique operational abilities, or other critical attributes. In such situations, the business is worth more to a particular key owner than it is to any other investors – unless the key person risks can be significantly reduced or eliminated.

The "special value" of your business may make it "priceless" to you. However, if your business is not transferable, it may be "valueless," or at least worth a great deal less to the other investors you need for successful ownership transitions.

Transferable Value

Our definition of transferable value relates to a company that has characteristics that other investors find attractive and are willing to pay for. I've often used the acronym of READY to provide a shorthand description of a business that has transferable value, or is ready for sale. READY is treated in more detail in Chapter 19, "Is Your Business Ready for Sale?"

- **R – Risks.** Specific risks, like key person risks or heavy customer concentrations, are minimized. Business value is a function of expected cash flow, risk, and growth (Value = Cash Flow / (R – G)). The R in the equation is the discount rate, which is reflective of the risks associated with a business. Since R is in the denominator of the fraction, if risks are reduced, then value increases, other things being equal. Given two businesses that are otherwise identical, the riskier one will sell for less and will probably take more time to sell.

> Our definition of transferable value relates to a company that has characteristics that other investors find attractive and are willing to pay for.

- **E – Earnings.** In the value equation (Value = Cash Flow / (R - G)), earnings are cash flow. A company that is ready for transfer or sale will have a good level of earnings relative to alternative investments in companies in the same industry. Increase expected cash flow, other things being equal, and the value and attractiveness of a business increases.

- **A – Attitudes, Aptitudes, Actions.** These three "A's" relate to the momentum of a business. Do you have attitudes, aptitudes and actions that foster good earnings and risk minimization? Are you working to get better at what you do and to provide better products or services? Other things being equal, a company that has momentum, or is positively moving in the direction of improvement on a continual basis, has more transferable value than one that is stagnant. Momentum has been defined as: "The rate of acceleration of a security's price or volume. The idea of momentum in securities is that their price is more likely to keep moving in the same direction" (www.investopedia.com). The same concept applies to closely held businesses.

- **D – Driving Growth.** Okay, I cheated. The relevant issue is growth but it doesn't hurt to be driving it. Remember the simple value equation above? G is in the denominator with a negative sign. If expected growth increases, the denominator decreases, and value increases. Other things being equal, a company that is growing faster than another will be more valuable and transferable than its slower-growing counterpart.

- **Y – Year-to-Year Comparisons.** How is your company doing relative to last year? Is it improving or deteriorating in performance? A company that is improving in performance, other things being equal, is more valuable and transferable than one that is experiencing a decline, if only temporary.

When you build transferable value in your business, you are creating potential opportunities to manage the private wealth being created. You can use the tools for managing private wealth discussed in Section II of this book.

Does your business have value to you? Does it have transferable value? Until the transferable value of your business is equal to or exceeds the value to you, you will be reluctant to engage in the logical transfer activities that are important for every business owner.

CHAPTER 15

10 Reasons That Businesses Change Ownership

To put the concept of business ownership into perspective, this chapter discusses ten reasons that business ownership changes hands. The list is not all-inclusive, but perhaps, as you read down the list, you will begin to see that this ownership transition thing could actually happen to you.

Why Do Businesses Change Hands?

1. **A primary owner dies unexpectedly.** That's it. It happens, and control passes. The owner isn't thinking about transitioning the ownership of his or her business, but death happens.

    We might ask a few questions here. To whom did ownership pass? Is there a buy-sell agreement that will dictate the pricing and terms of the ownership sale? Is life insurance in place to fund the purchase of this owner's shares? Were there appropriate plans in place to assure a smooth transition, not only of ownership, but of management, as well? These are things to think about while we are still alive. Otherwise, our families, fellow owners, key employees and others are left to sort things out under unfavorable and difficult circumstances.

2. **A key employee leaves.** This employee's departure could trigger the necessity to sell the entire business under unfavorable circumstances. This might be particularly true if this key person takes important contacts, critical energy, and/or leadership that keep things going and growing.

    A couple of questions to ask include: Does your business have such an employee or employees? Are these key employees subject to buy-sell agreements and/or employment agreements, if appropriate?

3. **The owner gets tired and decides to sell.** Tiredness is an unbelievably frequent reason why business ownership transfers occur. You may think that this circumstance might only happen with really small businesses and not with larger ones. Not so. Remember the A in READY from the last chapter. The attitudes, aptitudes, and actions that create momentum for a business apply to its owners, as well as employees.

    If you as a business owner wait until you are tired, you are already on the downside of the value curve. Tired owners almost unavoidably transmit their tiredness to employees and customers in many subtle ways. In the process, their businesses may lose vital force and momentum that is critical for ongoing growth and success.

4. **Unexpected offers come along.** Occasionally, a business owner receives an unexpected offer to purchase the business. When this occurs for a particular owner, he sometimes will sell to the surprise bidder or else decide then to put the company in play and sell to another, higher bidder.

    Was the business ready to be marketed? Was the owner ready for a transaction with his or her personal planning in place? Was the stock of the business distributed to family or other employees such that others could benefit appropriately? Just because someone comes along with a good price, even an outrageous price, does not mean that you are ready for ownership transition and sale.

5. **Business reversals happen.** Perhaps a company fails to adapt to changing markets, competition arises from unexpected quarters, or an accident or bad luck generates substantial losses. Sometimes the affected business never recovers and a forced sale results. This is obviously not a desirable outcome. Remember, bad things happen to even good companies.

6. **The primary owner divorces.** Marital dissolutions where closely held or family businesses are substantial marital assets occur with increasing frequency. Wild card divorce judgments can create settlement terms that are so onerous that a business needs to be sold to settle the marital estate.

    I once testified in a matter where the judge's solution to disagreements between a couple regarding their successful ($100 million) business was to force them to sell the entire business. Emotional changes resulting from the divorce can also create the necessity or the desire to sell the business.

7. **Life-changing experiences occur.** Business owners sometimes encounter life-changing experiences such as heart attacks, cancer, or close calls with death in accidents. We all experience the death of parents, spouses,

    Many of these questions and comments actually pertain to *owner readiness.*

    and friends. Such events can trigger significant changes in the desire to own and to manage a business. The emotional or physical shock of such experiences sometimes fosters a strong desire to "do things differently with the rest of my life." Business transfers can be the eventual results of these or other life-changing experiences.

8. **Gift and estate tax planning.** Owners of many successful, closely held and family businesses engage in gift and estate tax planning as a normal means of ownership transfer. Interestingly, the absence of proper gift and estate tax planning can precipitate the forced sale of a business if an owner's estate lacks the liquidity to handle estate taxes, or if a failure to plan for orderly and qualified management succession cripples the business when the owner is no longer there. See reason number one on this list above and think about your own estate tax planning.

9. **The second (or third or fourth) generation is not up to the task.** There is substantial research indicating that most family businesses do not survive to a second generation of family ownership. Further, some non-family businesses have a difficult time transitioning management to younger generations. Ability is one thing, but sometimes the next generation has no interest in running a business. Transition plans based on false expectations of a senior generation are bound to fail.

10. **Normal lifetime planning dictates timing.** Finally for this list, businesses sell as result of normal lifetime planning by their owners. These owners plan for and execute the sales of their businesses on their own timetables and terms. Numerous transfer mechanisms are employed in such transfers, including management buyouts (MBOs), Employee Stock Ownership Plans (ESOPs), leveraged recapitalizations, and other corporate finance techniques that are used to facilitate ownership transfer, in addition to outright sales. Quite often, such transfers occur over time while ownership and management are transferred in orderly fashion.

Are You Ready for Coming Transitions?

In the previous chapter, we introduced the acronym of READY to outline when a business is ready for sale. It talked about aspects of readiness, like reducing Risk, having Earnings and margins moving in the right direction, having good Attitudes and atmosphere conducive for growth, Driving growth, and having Year-to Year comparisons that are attractive to the market. The things we talked about in that chapter dealt conceptually, for the most part, with conditions in the business itself.

While this chapter has provided ten reasons that businesses change ownership, it should be clear that there are corollary issues for the key owners if they are to be ready for the eventual transfer of ownership in their businesses.

Many of these questions and comments actually pertain to *owner readiness*. There is no simple acronym, but it is clear that ownership readiness is a critical aspect of overall readiness for successful ownership and management transitions.

Recognize that ownership transitions will occur, perhaps unexpectedly, and you should be much more focused on taking action now to manage the wealth in your private business. The good things that need to happen well occur (or not) between your current status quo and any ultimate sale or disposition of your business. So, prepare for the unexpected.

CHAPTER 16

7 Ways the *Next Investors* Will Look at Your Business

There are at least seven ways that potential investors look at a business. Not every investor will look from every perspective. There are, of course, financial buyers and strategic buyers, and their perspectives will likely not be the same and not all perspectives will be relevant for every company. However, these various perspectives are worth discussing for your consideration.

The seven perspectives are particularly important in the context of implementing *The One Percent Solution* to help treat your business as the investment it is for you and your fellow owners.

How Do Investors Look at Businesses?

A number of years ago, I gave a talk to a group of business owners and was asked to address the question: "How do investors look at businesses?" They were not looking for specifics about profitability or margins or growth, but were asking about general ideas to facilitate their thinking. My first list had five perspectives and the list has now been expanded to seven. Here goes.

1. **At a point in time.** Your company's current balance sheet is a representation of the financial position of your business at a

point in time. However, understanding where you are at a point in time involves far more than taking a look at your balance sheet. After all, the next perspectives entail financial analysis that will examine your financial position.

Investors want to know more than financial position. They will want to visit your company and make a general assessment of how things look and even, on the softer side, "feel." How does your company present itself to the world? What is the state of your website? What are first appearances when coming to your offices? Your distribution facility? Your manufacturing facility? What is the appearance of any rolling stock or equipment used in your business?

For service companies, are your employees using current technology? What is the state of your operating and financial systems? Current? In need of upgrading or replacement? Do you have any significant customer concentrations? Product concentrations? Supplier concentrations? And on and on.

As you can see, there are first impressions regarding your business at a point in time and there are deeper impressions. It is important, then, to think like an investor as you look at your company currently. After all, you and your fellow owners are the current investors. So what is the condition of your company now, at this point in time? Don't let familiarity blind you to the first impressions of others.

2. **Relative to itself over time.** The beginning point of any business valuation is a financial spreadsheet analysis examining your business relative to itself over a period of several years. What trends are reflected on your income statements? Are sales growing, flattened out or declining? Are margins stable or improving?

What is happening with your top ten or twenty customers? What is happening with your top products or services? Are you creating new products and new services that are reflected in your income statements? What is your current financial position in relationship to your recent past?

Is your balance sheet excessively leveraged? How have your recent operations been perceived by your current lender(s)? Do you have excess assets on your balance sheet that no one other than you wants? How about excess working capital? What are your trends in receivables outstanding? How about payables?

If you are thinking like an investor, you will be watching the mentioned trends and others. As the current investors, you and your fellow owners are preparing your business for the next investors, which may be yourselves.

3. **Relative to peer groups.** Peer analysis is an important part of an investor's overall financial review of a business. Are your current margins at peer levels or above or below? What is the trend in your margins relative to the similar trends with your peer group? If your margins are well above your peer group, are they convincingly sustainable? Are the above-average margins the result of effective management or competitive advantage of some kind?

    Investors are sometimes concerned with a tendency for margins to experience what is called a "reversion to the mean" over time. If your margins are below peer levels, what is the explanation? If below peer levels, are your margins improving over time? Are there structural issues with your business that are hurting your margins, or are there "fixable" things that can be improved?

    What you don't want when you ultimately sell your business is for someone else to experience the favorable "reversion to the mean" that should have been available to you. Most businesses have some way of looking at peer groups, but it is sometimes easier to explain away unfavorable differences rather than to do something about them.

As the current investors, you and your fellow owners are looking at your relative performance, so are you acting to sustain advantage or to improve relatively adverse performance trends? The next investors will certainly do this.

4. **Relative to budget or plan.** Most successful and sizeable businesses have some form of operating budget or operating plan on an annual basis. How do you perform, over time, relative to your budget or operating plan?

    Let me illustrate from an experience in a litigation regarding business value. The other expert advanced a higher valuation conclusion in reliance on "management plans" for aggressive growth. When it was pointed out to the court that the CEO had had similar aggressive plans (or wishes) for the last several years that had not been achieved, the valuation question was resolved based on then current operations and a more reasonable outlook for the future.

    The next investors looking at your business will ask to look at your performance relative to plan in the past. As the current investors, you will want them to believe that they can experience a favorable future. Or, as in many transactions in the current environment, they may ask you to maintain an ongoing interest in the business. In any event, all investors are or should be interested in performance relative to plan, and in understanding reasons for significant under- or over-performance.

5. **Relative to your unique potential.** Many business owners want to believe that their companies are unique in the marketplace. Most companies, however, while they may be different in some ways from competitors, are not unique in the sense of one-of-a-kind uniqueness. So if your company indeed has a unique brand advantage or other competitive advantage, you will want the next investors to appreciate and pay for it. As the current investors, this means you need to realize this unique potential and take advantage of it.

6. **Relative to strategic or synergistic opportunities your platform offers.** When presenting companies to strategic investors, we always attempt to estimate or to anticipate the kinds of benefits that a client company might afford to them.

    The fact is that strategic or synergistic investors can view your earnings stream differently than you can as the current investor. There may be cost benefits from purchasing advantages or the ability to consolidate a portion of operations into larger business units. There may be revenue benefits from the ability to sell their products through your distribution channels or to sell your products through their channels. There may be other benefits, as well.

    If so, we want to highlight the cash flow difference in order to attempt to negotiate the benefit of all or a portion of that benefit for the selling investors. Not all companies are sold to strategic buyers. However, as the current investors, you and your fellow owners want to be aware of these potential benefits, if they exist.

7. **Relative to regulatory expectations or requirements.** For regulated companies like banks, insurance companies, many utilities and others, regulatory requirements establish certain operating rules that must be followed. The next investors for your business will obviously be aware of these requirements, if applicable.

167

For other companies, however, regulatory requirements may affect your business in the form of pension liabilities or environmental liabilities. And all future investors will want to know that you operate your business in compliance with all applicable laws and regulations, just as you want to know this as a current investor.

So there are at least seven perspectives that will be used by any future investors in your business to examine and analyze in their decisions to make investments in all or a portion of your stock.

What to Do Now?

Forewarned is, as they say, forearmed. This chapter is written from the viewpoint of *future investors* who may look at your business. But we have also talked about you and your fellow owners' perspectives as the *current investors* of your business. Since you now have an overview of how future buyers will look at your business if and when you decide to sell, it only makes sense to engage that future view in the present?

How can you do this? One way would be to have a qualified appraisal firm with transactional experience conduct a valuation analysis of your business that is geared to address the seven perspectives of future investors in more depth than might be employed in a typical appraisal. That analysis could highlight opportunities to reduce risk, and to enhance expected cash flow and growth.

You might consider having an annual appraisal. It would provide a number of *One Percent Solution* benefits as follows:

1. **Annual Appraisals and Monitoring of Performance.** Liquid assets are valued every day, and portfolio performance reports are made at least quarterly for most portfolios. Annual valuation is the best way of tracking investment performance over time, and for reporting to shareholders about a company's return performance relative to itself and to other asset categories.

I have been advocating the benefits of annual, or at least periodic, appraisal of businesses for many years. We now provide annual appraisals for more than 100 companies. Some of these companies have been clients for 25 or more years. There is clearly value in the process.

2. **Buy-Sell Agreement Pricing.** Annual valuations can also establish the value for buy-sell agreements. They are so important that I have written a print book (*Buy-Sell Agreements for Closely Held and Family Business Owners*) and an Amazon Kindle book (*Buy-Sell Agreements for Baby Boomer Business Owners*) about these critical and oft-ignored business agreements.

   In fact, the valuation process I most often recommend is that a single appraiser be agreed upon by the parties and employed to provide an initial valuation for buy-sell agreements, and then that the appraiser will provide annual revaluations to reset the price for the buy-sell agreement. Note that the annual appraisal for purposes of your buy-sell agreement could serve multiple purposes.

   > Forewarned is, as they say, forearmed. You might consider having an annual appraisal.

Any well-crafted appraisal will address many of the key issues outlined here. If you are not obtaining an annual (or periodic) appraisal, now is a good time to start. If you contact an appraiser, it would be good to begin with an in-depth valuation analysis like that outlined above as a starting point.

If you are already obtaining regular appraisals, it would be a good idea to ask your appraiser to conduct a more detailed valuation analysis from the viewpoint of future buyers. That analysis might be a separate document from your regular appraisal.

If *future investors* will assuredly be looking at your business from these seven perspectives, it is a pretty good idea for the *current investors* to do the same, at least periodically, and to make course adjustments if you see issues that would detract from future value from their perspective.

> If you are looking at your business the way that future investors will look at your business, you have an excellent perspective for considering the use of tools to help manage the wealth you are creating. After all, you and your fellow shareholders are the current investors. Think about it this way. Over time, as you grow the business and do not sell, you become the future investor in your business. This thought should change the way you think about your investment in your private business.

CHAPTER 17

Bad Things Happen to Good Companies

Bad things happen to even good companies, possibly even yours.

If you are a business owner, you may be thinking that diversification is not a good thing. You are, indeed, focused on the one basket represented by your investment in your business. And indeed, you should be focused on that basket. You are "concentrating to create" wealth. But you may also need to begin to "diversify to protect" your wealth.

You may be thinking that your investment in your business has achieved better returns than any other investment available to you, so why shouldn't you keep everything in that basket? After all, it has worked so far. Just remember this:

If you wait until it is too late to diversify, it will be too late.

This simple statement is powerfully true. As optimistic business owners, we tend to think that bad things happen, but to other people. So we wait to do things we know we should do. Financing that is readily available today to accomplish diversification objectives may not be available tomorrow. This can happen because of adverse events at your business, changes in the availability of financing, or both. Don't wait.

Concentrations Can be Risky and Value-Destroying

Why do we preach the benefits of diversification of private company wealth? In more than 30 years of working with business owners I have seen many bad things happen to otherwise good companies that had high or extreme concentrations of *something*. Those concentrations led to a variety of disasters, including:

- **Key customer loss.** A substantial business lost its dominant customer and was forced to liquidate. This business did not have a diversified portfolio of customers and the loss of one was sufficient to force it out of business.

- **Key supplier loss.** Another business purchased 80% of its products from a single supplier. When the supplier was purchased by a competitor, its supply chain was terminated. The company barely survived and it was never able to achieve even a fraction of its former sales and earnings.

- **Key owner/manager loss.** A business owner was key in all decision-making for his business. He trained no one and allowed no one to assume any real authority. Although the business was of substantial size, it rapidly deteriorated in sales, earnings and value in the months following his unexpected death.

- **Key product is outdated.** Another business had a dominant, single product line that is analog in nature. As technology advanced, this business never invested in newer product lines with advancing technologies. It now sells its single line of products to diminishing markets in the third world and is on a slow and painful decline that will likely never be reversed.

- **Key employee loss.** A company had a salesperson who was directly or indirectly responsible for more than 40% of its sales. The owners never tied this salesman to the company, either by contract or by making him an owner. They were shocked when he finally left to set up a competing business in the same city. He took several of the other salespersons with him along with 75% of their business.

This list (without details of the examples) sounds innocuous enough. However, the event at each company was far from innocuous when it happened. Each event was company-threatening, wealth-destroying, anxiety-provoking, and otherwise devastating for the owners and managers of the businesses. Bad things do happen to good companies.

A Valuation Perspective on Concentrations

What we've just seen regarding companies with concentrations can be examined from a valuation perspective. The value of a business is a function of its expected future cash flows (earnings), the expected growth of those cash flows, and the risks associated with achieving the future cash flows.

Using what is called the discounted cash flow model (DCF), we project expected future cash flows into the future and then, discount them to the present at an appropriate (risk-adjusted) discount rate.

The DCF model can be summarized by a single equation that will help illustrate why you should be concerned with diversifying concentrations (including wealth concentrations). You have seen this equation before.

$$\text{Value (V)} = \frac{\text{CF}}{(\text{R-G})}$$

Assume we have two companies that are alike in all respects such as revenues, margins, cash flow and everything else – except for the following.

One company has 50 customers with no single customer providing more than 5% of revenues. The other has 100 customers, but one customer provides about 60% of its sales.

In this example, the R, or discount rate for the second company would definitely be higher than for the first. It is riskier and buyers and appraisers recognize this. Therefore, even with all other things being equal except for customer concentration, the second company will be worth less than, likely a good bit less than, the first.

Why do we preach the benefits of diversification of private company wealth? In more than 30 years of working with business owners I have seen many bad things happen to otherwise good companies that had high or extreme concentrations of *something*.

R (the discount rate reflecting risk) is in the denominator of the bottom equation above, so the math illustrates the common sense. If R, or risk, increases with other things remaining the same, V, or value, will decline.

In essence, investors do a form of anticipation of the bad things that can happen to good companies when they assess the potential impact of customer concentrations, supplier concentrations, and other risks in their determinations of offering prices. Business appraisers do the same thing in the process of valuing businesses.

As we have discussed in the concept of *The One Percent Solution,* it is important to work on your business over time while beginning a disciplined process of wealth diversification outside the business. If, for example, you know you have a concentration risk that is currently having a dampening impact on your company's value, you can increase its value by working to reduce that concentration over time.

Regulatory and Accounting Changes

Customer and other concentrations aside, other things can change adversely. But good things can happen as well. The following example is but one of them. As you will see, it is somewhat personal in nature.

Regulatory Change

President George Bush signed the Economic Growth and Tax Relief Reconciliation Act of 2001 in early 2001. One of the features of this act was the so-called "repeal" of the estate tax. The act had adverse consequences for any companies or service providers who were involved with assisting business owners and other clients with gift and estate tax planning. Sounds innocuous enough, but change can get personal.

With the stroke of President Bush's pen, about 50% of nearly 50% of the revenue of my firm, Mercer Capital, disappeared, and almost instantly. We were heavily concentrated in providing valuation services associated with gift and estate tax planning. That was almost 25% of our annual revenue! That was bad news, but it didn't turn out as bad as it might have been. A number of valuation firms with concentrations in the gift and estate planning area simply went out of business.

Accounting Change

Fortunately, another change was underway, which brought good news. During 2000 and 2001, the Financial Accounting Standards Board (FASB) was publicly in the process of issuing a statement to supersede Statement No. 121, Accounting for the Impairment of Long-Lived Assets and for Long Lived Assets to Be Disposed of. Whew!

Statement No. 144, Accounting for the Impairment or Disposal of Long Lived Assets was in process and was finalized in August 2001. It was effective for companies filing financial statements after December

15, 2001, with some companies electing early adoption. Statement No. 144 required that goodwill on companies' balance sheets be "tested" for impairment, which basically created a new valuation requirement for many companies, much of which work was likely to be performed by independent firms like Mercer Capital.

While still reeling from the tax regulatory change and its impact on our company, we did respond, and almost instantly, to counter the adverse change. Our younger leaders identified revenue replacement potential in the then-emerging financial statement reporting business, which was a direct result of the pending issuance of Statement No. 144.

They conceived the idea of writing a book, *Valuation for Impairment Testing*, that went from thought to publication in 75 days. Fear of loss can be a strong motivator. We shipped it by FedEx to 2,500 accounting firm partners and CFOs of companies in perhaps ten states and we were instantly in the financial statement reporting valuation business – and still are.

Aggressive action on their part helped mitigate a good bit of the revenue loss from gift and estate tax planning. We ultimately had a decent and profitable year in 2001, although performance was down somewhat. Our financial statements, however, like the stories above, did not convey the angst of dealing with that year.

Good things can happen from bad things. The young leaders who stepped up then are now the senior management of our firm. However, as the stories above illustrate, the outcomes from the adverse impact of concentrations are not always so favorable. We were lucky. We no longer have so much concentration in any line of business – and certainly no concentrations of clients. We learned our lesson.

I could go on, but I think you get the picture.

Yes, but...

You may be thinking that nothing like the above could happen to your company. Think some more. Bad things happen to good people and bad things happen to good companies.

When (or if) that time comes for your business, you will want to have sufficient assets set aside so that you can live comfortably and independently of your business. Remember, when it is too late to diversify, it is too late.

A time of reversal in your business is not a good time to attempt to sell. Selling following adverse events or amidst adverse trends puts you in the position of what I call "Yes, but..." selling.

- Question: "Didn't you just lose your largest customer?"

  Answer: "Yes, but you can find another..."

- Question: "So, your best salesman just left and took 20% of your business?"

  Answer: "Yes, but we'll get those customers back and more..."

- Question: Your margins have been declining for the last three years?

  Answer: "Yes, but I'm sure you can turn them around..."

You get the picture.

Conclusion

Use the tools for managing private wealth from Section II in the interim, between your current status quo and any ultimate sale or disposition of your company.

When you do transfer, you want to be sure you have sufficient assets to provide the lifestyle and legacy that you intend for your family, for charity, or for other purposes you deem important.

The only way to be sure that this will happen is to plan for the important transitions in business and in life and to manage your wealth so that it will be available when you need it.

As we saw in the Ownership Transfer Matrix in previous chapters, you will transfer your business – it is just a matter of when and how. You will do so in whole or in part, and either voluntarily or involuntarily. So a major focus of this book is to encourage you to take voluntary action under favorable circumstances and with timing of your choosing. Again, bad things do happen to good companies, so it pays to be prepared.

CHAPTER 18

10 Thoughts on CEO Management Succession for Private Companies

Marshall Goldsmith, the author and executive coach, wrote a little (in size only) book entitled *Succession: Are You Ready?* (Cambridge, Harvard Business Press, 2009). In it, he talks about letting go and moving on. His words should be taken to heart by many, if not most of us:

> *Almost all of the leaders who I have met assure me that they will be different. They confidently assert that they will have no problems letting go. You are probably delusional enough to believe that you too will be different. Take my word for it: while your desire for uniqueness may be theoretically possible, it is statistically unlikely.*

How business owners address the issue of management succession is vital to the success of business transitions and it is one that too often receives scant attention.

One of the most difficult things to realize is that we all have to let go. We have to let go of things throughout our lives in order to make room for newer and better things.

Management transitions are difficult for many baby boomer business owners. It is just difficult to imagine your company without you in charge. But life is better on the other side. You will transition and, as Marshall Goldsmith notes, you will likely have problems letting go.

Public Companies Should But Don't Always Get CEO Succession Right

There is a great deal of news about management succession for public companies. Every change is recorded publicly and the changes are analyzed in a variety of ways. In a typical year, 8-10% of public company CEOs in the United States change. Over half of the incoming CEOs are from outside the company where change is occurring. This means that more than half of the companies failed to develop a workable succession plan.

Private Companies are Somewhat Different

Unlike public companies, closely held and family businesses do not typically have an external mandate (i.e., public shareholders, bond holders and other stakeholders) to plan for CEO and key management succession. Granted, there is responsibility there, but it is, for the most part, internally based. Take this a step further and consider the many businesses founded by or inherited by baby boomers.

Many baby boomers have been CEO of their companies for so long they cannot imagine life and not being the person in charge. Many of the companies have never had a change in the CEO, so there is no history and no model to follow. In most instances, there is no immediate pressure for change, since things are running along fairly smoothly. So nothing happens, and no one says or does anything.

The problem is exacerbated because many business founders/owners find it difficult to step outside themselves and look at their businesses objectively. If they could, they would see the need (or past due need) to initiate a workable plan for management and ownership succession.

Poor CEO succession planning can erode value in public companies, but, at least many of them have bench depth in managers running their various subsidiaries or operating divisions. They also have boards of directors who will step in and take charge when forced to do so by circumstances.

Private companies tend to be somewhat different. They may lack bench depth in their management structure. Their boards may be weak and controlled by the owner/CEOs, who may not be interested in planning. Value can be eroded, perhaps quickly, if something happens to the existing CEO in the absence of a plan for succession.

10 Thoughts on Private Company Management Succession

I am not a management succession consultant, although I've worked with a handful of companies over the years to assist with management transition planning. What follows are a series of thoughts based on my personal reading and personal experiences as they relate to successful management succession planning and implementation. This is written directly to CEOs who need to think about the necessary management transition processes for themselves and for their companies.

1. **Transition before it is necessary.** Over the years, we have seen many, many successful closely held and family businesses where the founder and/or CEO simply would not yield the title and function to capable younger managers. There are many stories of CEOs who hang on too long and fail to provide growth opportunities for their children in the business or for their younger managers. In a number of cases, the CEO has died in the saddle, leaving the company without strong leadership and without an organized plan for succession. The results range from disruption to disaster.

2. **Transition before you are ready.** If you wait for that magic moment when you are ready to make a transition, the moment may never come. There are always things to be done and reasons to procrastinate. Do you need to let go, or to begin to let go now?

3. **Link leadership development with succession planning.** Over time, leadership skills are gained or emerge. In many companies, natural leaders emerge for a variety of reasons. The long-range process of leadership development for key persons in any company provides valuable input into the management succession process.

4. **Share knowledge with your senior team.** Call it coaching or leadership development, it is a good idea to share knowledge and experience with the senior members of management from which the new CEO will likely come. Travel together, meet with clients together, go to meetings together, and so on. As CEO, you may be older than most of the members of your team. They need to learn from your experiences and you need to learn from theirs. It is through this process that you become comfortable with each other and with your ultimate decision for successor CEO.

5. **Consider potential successors.** Most private companies tend to look within for successors, so it is good to be evaluating potential candidates for the new CEO. If you are in a process of evaluating, you can give special projects or assignments to the various candidates along the way. At some point, hopefully, the choice becomes clear. At some point, hopefully, you and your board of directors must decide on one candidate to lead the business. When you feel the time is right, then make the decision.

6. **Set an emergency plan into place.** While an owner/CEO may be healthy, happy and productive, bad things happen to healthy, happy and productive people. Every business owner needs to

have a will that specifies what will happen to his or her estate upon death. Every business should also have an emergency succession plan, even if it is acknowledged to be temporary in nature, in the event of the untimely death or disability of the CEO. It is easier on everyone if there is a temporary plan already in place.

7. **Succession planning is a risk management function.** From the points outlined above, it should be clear that succession planning is a way to anticipate and to reduce the impact of the risks to an organization that can damage it based on untimely or emergency succession requirements. Remember the basic valuation equation. Lower risk (in the denominator of $V = CF / (R - G)$), other things being equal, tends to increase value.

8. **Avoid the "just like me" trap.** There are a number of reasons to avoid looking for a successor CEO that is like you. First, you might just not get along if you are too much alike. Second, if he or she is just like you, he or she will have the same weaknesses and issues that you have. In all likelihood, your company needs a change. Third, you are the CEO that has brought the company from startup, or from wherever when you came on board, to its present situation. Does someone just like you have the skills and attitudes necessary to take the company to its expected better future? Using Marshall Goldsmith's line, that may be theoretically possible, but it is statistically unlikely.

> We have to let go of things throughout our lives in order to make room for newer and better things.

9. **Develop a succession plan and don't wait on events.** An event-driven CEO succession in a public company is often an unsuccessful process, even with active boards of directors, bench strength in management, and perhaps a history of

working through such events in the past. In a private company, an event-driven change, such as the death or disability of the owner/CEO, can be disastrous. Most private companies don't have active boards, excess management depth or experience with succession. If your board, management team, other owners and employees are faced with such an event, no one knows how or how quickly or effectively they will respond. It is far better to have a succession plan in place, even an emergency plan as noted above.

10. **Figure out the ongoing role for the old CEO.** In many public companies, when the now CEO is named, the former CEO rides off into the proverbial sunset. In my experience, in closely held and family businesses, the old CEO is highly likely to stay around in some capacity. If he stays and meddles, then the likelihood of success is lowered. If he stays and performs an agreed-upon role for the company that does not involve micromanaging the new CEO, then good things can happen.

Management transition is inevitable. Business owners should view transition as part of the private company wealth management process. Your company will be much more attractive to potential future investors if you have successfully transitioned management and found an appropriate role for yourself, either in the company or elsewhere.

CHAPTER 19

Is Your Business Ready for Sale?

We have talked several times about ways to diversify wealth from the base of successful closely held and family businesses. Many of the methods discussed, like dividend policy, special dividends, leveraged dividends and leveraged share repurchases, specifically do not involve the sale of an entire business. I am not an advocate of anyone selling a business unless it is the right time and thing to do or, in some instances, the only thing to do. However, it is a good idea to be sure that your business is ready for sale at any time.

We just don't know when the time will be right or when an irresistible offer will come along. If your business is not ready for sale when such opportunities arise, you will miss out on significant potential benefits in a lower than ideal purchase price.

In my experience, a business that is ready for sale is, first of all, lots more fun to work in than one that is not ready. And a business that is ready for sale is, well, ready for sale if an appropriate opportunity comes along or when it is appropriate to engage in a partial sale (or purchase) of a portion of the business through the judicious use of leverage.

Is Your Business READY?

READY, a tool, or filter, through which to look at your business was introduced in Chapter 14. Let's now ask the question: Is Your business READY for sale?

R stands for **Risk**
E stands for **Earnings, or EBITDA**
A stands for **Attitudes, Aptitudes, and Activities**
D stands for **Driving Growth**
Y stands for **Year-to-Year Comparisons**

As we begin to talk about READY, recall that business value is all about expected cash flow, the expected growth of cash flow, and the risks associated with achieving the expected cash flows. This flows from the basic valuation formula:

$$\text{Value (V)} = \frac{\text{CF}}{(\text{R-G})}$$

We relate the components of the valuation formula to illustrate how the concept of READY helps keep focus on building value.

The R in READY Stands for Risk

The algebra of risk is quite straightforward in the basic valuation formula. R, the discount rate, is in the denominator of the equation. Increasing risk therefore decreases value, other things being equal. However, the equation works both ways – decreasing risk, other things being equal, increases value.

At the outset, as we talk about risk in business, let's agree that there are two kinds of risks – those we can do something about (controllable) and those we can't do anything about (uncontrollable). It may seem obvious, but as business owners and managers, it is far more productive to work on controllable risks than to worry about uncontrollable risks.

Uncontrollable risks relate to the level and direction of the national, regional or local economies, the level and direction of movement of interest rates, industry conditions, and the general availability of financing, among other factors.

Controllable risks relate to everything else. But remember the famous quote from George Orwell's *Animal Farm*: "All animals are equal, but some animals are more equal than others." Similarly, all controllable risks are controllable, but some are more controllable than others. It is therefore wise to focus initially on reducing risks where management can have the most direct impact in the short run, and to address other risks over time.

Some of the most obvious risks in businesses relate to concentrations. Businesses can be concentrated in a variety of ways as was discussed in Chapter 17.

Customer concentration is one that obviously comes to mind. Other concentrations can be in products, markets, suppliers, locations, sales persons, managers (key persons) and others.

Still other risks can impact value. For example, there is a correlation between market multiples and size. Larger companies are perceived to be less risky than smaller ones. Leveraged companies tend to be more risky than are well-financed businesses (although some theorists will tell you that leverage won't impact the value of a firm). Rising leverage tends to reduce options, which can increase risk.

Let's go back to the topic of customers for a minute as we conclude this short discussion of risk. Years ago, I worked with a very successful stockbroker by the name of Wally Lowenbaum. We were traveling in England visiting Wally's institutional customers to talk about (sell) bank stocks and were having dinner one evening. I asked him: "Wally, what is the secret of your success?"

Wally responded, "Chris, I'd have to say that there are two things that I think about all the time. The first is momentum. If you don't have momentum in your business, you have to do everything in your power to get it. And if you have it, you have to do everything in your power to maintain it. Momentum is a critical key to success!

The second key to success is customers. You can't make money without customers, and too many brokers [substitute your industry] lose too many customers to really succeed."

I asked Wally, "Well, how do you keep customers?"

Wally replied, "Chris, most brokers [substitute your industry] don't lose customers because they lose money for their customers. If you're in the brokerage business, that is going to happen. Most brokers lose customers because they ignore them while they lose money for them! Brokers who work with their clients in good times and bad will tend to keep them, and that is exactly what I try to do."

Personally, I've never forgotten this advice, and I've tried to follow it ever since – and this dinner occurred in 1980. Wally was all about not being complacent in your business.

So remember that the R in READY stands for Risk. If you can reduce risk, all other things remaining the same, you can increase value, make your business more attractive to potential buyers, and continue the process of getting or maintaining your business in a ready for sale mode.

The E in READY Refers to EBITDA (Earnings)

Earnings are important to business valuation. Remember the CF, or cash flow, in the basic earnings equation. Cash flow is in the numerator, so an increase in expected cash flow, other things being equal, will increase the value of a business. As we talk about earnings, we will talk about EBITDA. EBITDA is the broadest measure of earnings to look at, and it is considered to be important by everyone who buys companies. Interestingly, you will not find EBITDA on your company's financial statement. It is a derived earnings concept. So what does EBITDA mean?

Earnings Before Interest, Taxes, Depreciation and Amortization

Think about EBITDA by beginning with pre-tax income, which is precisely total revenue minus total costs (except taxes). Now, add interest expense, the payments you make for borrowed funds, depreciation, which is a non-cash charge to replenish your investments in fixed assets, and amortization, which is a non-cash charge to amortize any depreciable intangible items on your balance sheet.

When buyers begin with EBITDA, they are thinking in terms of gross cash flow available from a business to meet all obligations and to provide a return on the capital invested in it. When we talk about buyers, we are talking about the most likely buyers for businesses of any size, either private equity funds or other companies.

From the EBITDA base level of cash flow, buyers can begin to make decisions about how to utilize that cash flow in an acquisition. In other words, if they have a handle on the capacity of your business to generate EBITDA, they can assess:

- What their capital expenditure requirements will be.

- Capital expenditure requirements can be assessed in light of a Company's EBITDA.

- How much debt they can safely carry in an acquisition? In other words, they can estimate, at prevailing interest rates and borrowing terms, the amount of debt-service they can handle (principal and interest).

- Interest expense and depreciation are tax-deductible, so they can then estimate their net income and capacity to pay down debt over time and maintaining momentum.

- Then, given the amount of their equity contributions to the deal and the structure of their financing, they can calculate their expected return on investment, probably using some form of internal rate of return analysis.

The forecasts of expected returns, in relationship to the expectations that various buyers have for future returns, i.e., their required returns or discount rates, establish the relevant range of pricing that rational, financial buyers are likely to pay.

This process just described is the manner in which the market determines whether your company will be worth, in terms of multiples of EBITDA, 4x, 5x, or 6x, or more, or less — or much more, or much less. A little competition among buyers who find your company attractive will also help.

So, when we say to focus on Earnings, or EBITDA, there are very good reasons for you to do so.

The A in READY Stands for Attitudes, Aptitudes, and Activities

I'm cheating a bit because the A in READY is all about the people and momentum in your organization. We can ask a number of good questions for you to think about:

- Are the right people in place?

- Are they doing what they should be doing?

- Are they doing it when and where they should be doing it?

- Are they doing it with whom they should be doing it?

Other critical questions to ask and to work on over time include:

- What is the attitude and culture in your business regarding customer service?

- What is the attitude and culture in your business on product or service quality?

- What is the attitude and culture in your business regarding sales?

Years ago, I got out of the Army while still stationed in Europe and traveled for a while. When I returned to the States, I was traveling through New York on the way back to Tennessee and I happened to read an issue of the *Wall Street Journal*. There was a large box of white space on a page that included only these words: "It's not creative unless it sells."

As you think about getting your business ready for sale, remember, "SELL is not a four-letter word!" Write that one down and remember it. You'll find it a helpful reminder as you spend time with your customers and employees.

The bottom line of the A in READY is that in terms of Attitudes, Aptitudes, and Activities, we need to be focused on having our people in the right places doing the right things over time.

The D in READY Stands for Driving Growth

Remembering our basic equation of (Value = CF / (R-G)), it should be clear that there is a direct relationship between growth and value (because raising G with a negative sign decreases the denominator which increases value). Generally speaking, the more rapid your company is expected to grow into the future, the more favorably buyers will look at your prospects and reflect those expectations into their pricing.

Recall the familiar saying: "Rising tides lift all boats." Sometimes companies find themselves in industry conditions or individual circumstances where, for periods of time, growth seems easy, or relatively easy. That's wonderful when it happens to you. Do everything in your power to maintain that momentum. But don't fall into the trap of believing you are really good when it is primarily the rising industry tide that is lifting your boat. It will be that much more difficult to adapt when the tide goes out.

Unfortunately, many business do not find themselves in situations where growth seems easy. So how do we drive growth when the tide isn't rising? Here are a few things to think about.

- **Make growth an intentional goal.** Companies grow through tougher times because their management teams are intentional about growth and stay focused on that goal. Growth does not happen for most businesses absent conscious decisions on the part of the owners and/or key managers.

- **Focus on customer needs and customer service and customer profitability.** Recall the old adage of business success: "Find a need and fill it." Your customers have needs and you will grow by satisfying those needs. At the margin, this means recognizing emerging needs and satisfying them before your competitors do. Customer service is king. Is your business focused on customer service at every point of contact, from initial calls, to returning calls, to simply thanking customers for their business? Customer profitability is also important. In many businesses, a disproportionate share of revenues and profits come from a relatively few customers. Are you doing business with enough of the kinds of customers that can provide good profitability and therefore drive growth? In the period before "upsizing" orders, McDonald's trained its staff to ask a question every time, "Would you like fries with that?" Many businesses would benefit from asking their version of that questions to their own customers.

- **Make technology work for you.** Technology is important in nearly every area of most companies. Are your products and services current, up-to-date, and reflective of customer expectations? Are your services delivered using current technology? Technology impacts how services are delivered and how your services are perceived by customers and clients. I've had an expression for years that we want to be on the leading, but not the bleeding, edge of technology in our business. Where are you?

- **Be intentional about hiring and retaining the best people.** A business cannot grow without the right people doing the right things over time. Investing in people won't guarantee that your business will grow, but not investing will virtually assure that it will not grow. Don Hutson, a nationally known motivational speaker and sales trainer, tells the story of an executive who asked this question in the process of initiating a significant sales training program. "What if we spend all this money and they leave?" Don's response was simply this: "What if we don't and they stay!" Hire the best people you can find, train them and retain them.

Growth is important for all businesses. Not only does profitable growth enhance business value, but it also rejuvenates and energizes companies and their people.

The Y in READY Stands for Year-to-Year Comparisons

Most businesses generate financial statements on a monthly basis, very often on a quarterly basis, and always on an annual basis. Financial statements are generally produced for key subsidiaries or divisions, and on a consolidated basis for complex organizations.

Companies also produce operational statements tracking key aspects of their operations, including year-to-year sales, product and customer profitability, branch or location profitability, as well as statements measuring various aspects of flow-through and productivity.

It is a good idea to be sure that your business is ready for sale at any time.

In other words, the typical business generates a lot of numbers. Years ago, I was assistant treasurer at First Tennessee National Corporation, now First Horizon. My boss and mentor was the bank's CFO, Bob Rogers, an astute businessman and keen financial analyst. Bob told me on many occasions, "Chris, you've got to talk to the numbers until the numbers talk to you." It took me a while to understand what he meant. The numbers of a business are the summary representations of the activities of the business, and the best measure of the results of those activities, as measured in a variety of ways.

So I learned that a good analyst could, in many instances, understand, or at least make educated guesses, about what has actually happened in a company historically because of the way that those activities are represented in its financial statements.

For example, I was once asked to perform a blind analysis of a bank with no contact with its management. I was able to describe for my clients what had happened, as well as to describe the management philosophy and style of the bank's CEO. How could I do that? Well, the numbers talked to me. The point is that your numbers can talk to you – and if not you, then to trusted members of your management team and/or advisers.

Too often, business owners and managers fall into the trap of looking only at the most current financial and operating statements. That will tell what things look like at a point in time, and likely, at the same point in time last year, but that is not enough.

Trends are of critical importance in your business. Rest assured, when buyers look at your business, they will look at more than the current period, whether this month, quarter, or year. They will look at your historical performance in a variety of ways. Importantly, they will be looking at the past to provide a window through which they can gauge the prospects for expected future cash flow. You want that window to be clean and as clean as possible

Good results, being defined as steady progress, consistent margins, strong productivity, and growing earnings do not happen by chance. Management is all about making results happen.

The concept of year-to-year comparisons will help keep you focused on the key trends that impact, not only the value of your business and its attractiveness for sale, but also the fun and pleasure that can be derived from building a growing, successful business.

The short point of the Y of READY, Year-to-Year comparisons, is that the record of your business, the one that you and your shareholders live with every quarter, is being created right now. At a future point in time, when you are ready or need to sell, buyers will be looking at the record you have created up to that point in time. It is that record that will help set the expectations for the future they can envision with your business.

Is Your Business Ready for Sale?

"Is your business ready for sale?" is a question that is important for your business and its owners. Reasons for insuring that your business is constantly READY, or in the process of becoming READY for sale include:

- Companies that are READY for sale are more valuable than similar companies that are not.

- You never know when you might be approached by an enthusiastic, or better yet, a motivated purchaser. If that day comes unexpectedly, you definitely want to be READY for sale.

- A company that is READY for sale is also ready to engage in leveraged repurchase transactions that provide liquidity for some owners and enhanced returns for others.

- A company that is READY for sale is capable of engaging in a leveraged dividend recapitalization, as well, to provide liquidity and diversification opportunities for all shareholders.

- Companies that are READY for sale are also just more fun to work in than those that are not.

So, Is your business READY for sale? Remember, we are not talking about your business being up for sale, just READY. From the viewpoint of managing the wealth in your private company, the concept of READY for sale may be the most important perspective of all.

CHAPTER 20

25 Questions for Business Owners

We have been asking questions as we have developed the message of this book. However, a series of probing questions provides an excellent end to our book.

The following is a list of 25 questions to think about in assessing whether you as an owner are treating your business as an investment. If you are a business adviser, you can ask the questions on your clients' behalf or, better still, in meetings with them.

1.   How much is your closely held or family business worth?

How much is your interest in the business worth if you own less than all of its shares (or other interests)? Having asked the question, the truth is that what you think doesn't matter. All that matters is: 1) what a buyer of capacity thinks if and when you are ready

How much money will you need to live the lifestyle you desire when you are no longer working and receiving a salary?

to sell your business; or, 2) what a qualified business appraiser thinks in the interim and will express in a valuation report for an ESOP, a buy-sell agreement, a gifting plan, for the estate of an owner, or whenever independent corroboration is needed for interim transactions.

2. **How do you know what your business is worth? Has it been independently valued in the last three years?**

As discussed several times previously, I recommend that every successful closely held and family business have an appraisal each year, or at least every other year. If you can do this, you will have the best information available about the value for your private company.

3. **What portion of your personal net worth is represented by your business ownership interest?**

If you will just make a calculation with whatever estimate you have of your company's worth in relationship to your other assets, you will likely be surprised at how concentrated your wealth is. For Mr. Jones in our ongoing example, the answer is 80%, or quite concentrated. What are the answers for you and for your other key owners?

4. **What has been your shareholders' rate of return on their investment over the last one, two, three, four, or five years or more?**

Return on investment (ROI) is not something that many private business owners talk about. Simply, an investment in a business provides returns in two forms, interim distributions (after taxes) and capital gains, or the appreciation in the value of the investment each year and over time. And don't forget, above market owner compensation and other expensive perquisites are part of your return on investment.

5. **How does this rate of return performance compare with alternative investments, e.g., in the public securities markets?**

You almost certainly know how your professionally managed liquid funds are performing. After all, you get a report from your manager at least quarterly, and perhaps more frequently. Have you ever compared your return on your business with that of your liquid wealth? You might be surprised, either pleasantly or not, if you have the information.

6. **Is your wealth adequately diversified to avoid the risk of major losses from adverse events with any of your assets, including your business?**

Rephrasing the question, if your business suffered a major loss of value, do you have sufficient assets outside the business to sustain a reasonable lifestyle? For many business owners, the answer is no. And for owners who build lifestyles based on their returns to labor (salary and benefits) *and* the economic distributions of their businesses, the answer is likely no.

7. **Do you know how to increase your company's value over time?**

You have been successful so far. Do you know and are you working on things to do to increase the value of your business over time? Even with large, highly successful businesses, significant enhancements in valuation can occur through efforts to reduce risk, to facilitate cash flow, and to use the balance sheet in a prudent manner.

8. **Are you working your way out of being a key person in your business?**

What would happen if you went to the beach and didn't come back? Have you designated someone to run the business in your absence or if you are unavailable?

9. **How much money will you need to live the lifestyle you desire when you are no longer working and receiving a salary?**

Pull out the calculator or have your financial adviser do it for you. What income will be required to support you when you are not working in the business? That's pretty easy to figure, probably based on your current lifestyle. How many dollars do you need invested at 4%, 5% or 6% such that you can generate that income from passive assets? Do you have other sources of income? These are important question and they deserve your attention.

10. **Does your business make economic distributions (in excess of those necessary to pay taxes)?**

If your business is profitable and achieves a reasonable return on equity and is not growing very fast, then you should be able to make economic distributions, or distributions after paying income taxes (assuming you have a pass-through entity). These economic distributions become an ongoing source for accumulating wealth outside your business.

11. **If you are not making economic distributions, is the return on your reinvestment of earnings into fixed assets or working capital or technology or whatever sufficient to warrant the investments?**

If you have to reinvest all of the company's earnings and you are not growing steadily, something may be wrong and you are likely not achieving a reasonable return on your investment in the business.

12. **Are you reinvesting distributions in diversified assets as part of a plan to diversify your wealth? If not, why not?**

This point follows up on the previous question about distributions. It can be a mistake to believe that distributions are a part of your earned income and fully available to support lifestyle.

Your business provides you with three forms of return if you work there. First, you receive your salary, normal bonus and benefits. This is the return on your labor. Any distribution in excess of that, even if it comes in the form of additional bonus, is the income return from your investment in the business. The final form of return is the appreciation in the value of your investment from year to year. Too often, owners in even substantial businesses do not make this important distinction between returns to labor and returns on investment.

13. What is the plan to obtain liquidity from your ownership of your business?

If your plan is to wait until some indefinite time in the future when you hope to sell the business, that may not be a plan but a wish. Begin to think about employing some of the ideas found in this book to generate liquid assets from your business. The interim, i.e., the time between now and that indefinite time when you wish to sell, can offer lots of surprises and lots of benefits.

14. What is the plan for the other shareholders, if any, to obtain liquidity from their investments?

Many successful closely held and family businesses have multiple shareholders, often with owners in different generations. This is true whether the owners are all in one family or not. Assume you are in charge with a significant stake. The point I made about distributions above holds true here. Minority owners not working in the business do not receive a return on labor from the business. But they are entitled to distributions or opportunities for liquidity at appropriate times. Share repurchases along the way can provide significant return enhancements for longer-term owners. But you have to realize that the other owners are, well, owners, and are entitled to their returns on investment just like you.

15. **Are the plans for liquidity realistic and documented?**

Do your other owners know about your plans? Does your family know about your plans? The Law of Unintended Consequences deals harshly with the unprepared.

16. **Is your business "ready for sale" whether or not you have any interest in selling today?**

When we talk about having a business "ready for sale," we do not talk about necessarily preparing for an actual sale. Most business sales occur rather unexpectedly. So if you might sell your business unexpectedly this year, next year, or the next year, why not keep it in a position of readiness for sale? A business that is ready for sale has decent margins, is growing, lacks large customer or other concentration risks, and is focused on management and ownership transitions. Why not be "ready for sale" all the time. We guarantee that a business in that ongoing state is a lot more fun and profitable to run than otherwise.

17. **Are there things you know that need to be done and that take time to begin to get the business in a position to be "ready for sale?"**

This question could cause you to think about obvious concentrations in your business. If you have an overhang of stale inventory, get rid of it now so there will be no question later. If you need to train and appoint a successor COO, then be in the process of doing so. It is so much easier to work on these and other issues on your own time. It is almost impossible when you are attempting to sell, and they will drag down value and proceeds.

18. **What are the plans to transfer ownership and/or management to other members of your family or to others not in your family or in the family of a co-owner?**

Is there a plan for management transition? Is there a plan for ownership transition? Are these plans documented and do the right people know about them?

19. Are the ownership and management transition plans realistic? Do those you are thinking about know about and agree with your plans?

You know what your stock ownership is currently. What do you and other key owners think that the ownership distribution should be in one year, two years, or five years. It won't change by chance. Regarding management transitions, it is far better to move them along sooner rather than later in most instances. The longer your business is highly dependent on you or you and a partner or two, the harder it will be to change as time progresses.

20. Does your company have a buy-sell agreement? If so, how do you know that it will work if or when it is triggered?

If the buy-sell agreement has a fixed price, is it realistic and current? How do you know? If the plan depends on a formula to price agreement transactions, is the formula realistic in current market and financing conditions? Has anyone calculated it recently? What are the provisions for adjusting the formula for known issues like non-recurring costs or income items? If the plan calls for multiple appraisers, do you know what will happen when it is triggered? Most buy-sell agreements are ticking time bombs and will likely not provide reasonable resolutions. Our suggestion to the owners of successful closely held and family businesses is that they revise their buy-sell agreements such that they agree to the following. Select a single appraiser now. Have that appraiser provide a draft appraisal now. All parties review the draft now to be sure that the appraiser has interpreted the valuation language in the buy-sell agreement the way the owners are thinking, and then finalize the valuation. This becomes the price for the agreement until the next reappraisal, which establishes a new price. And so on. We recommend this because it works. It avoids confusion, litigation and angst when trigger events occur. It provides certainty as to the process. For a quick look at the details, go to Amazon and purchase *Buy-Sell Agreements for Baby Boomer Business Owners* for your Kindle or Kindle app.

21. **If there is life insurance associated with a buy-sell agreement, are the instructions within the buy-sell agreement and in any related documents clear as to how any proceeds of life insurance proceeds will be treated for valuation purposes?**

Life insurance can be considered as a funding vehicle. If so, the insurance proceeds are not considered part of company value and are used to acquire the stock of a deceased owner. Life insurance proceeds can also be considered to be a corporate asset. Under this treatment, the proceeds are added to value dollar-for-dollar before the per share price for the estate is determined. The choice of treatments can make a substantial difference in results for a selling shareholder, the company and the remaining shareholders. If there is life insurance associated with your agreement, be sure that the agreement specifies its use in unambiguous terms. If the treatment is ambiguous or not present in the agreement, there will almost certainly be disagreement between the estate and the company and other owners. It is easier to agree when all the parties are in the here and now. It is virtually impossible to agree when one of the parties is in the hereafter.

22. **Is your will current and does it reflect your current intentions for what happens in the event of your death?**

I am not an estate planner, but this is a basic issue. The time of one's death is tough on the family. It is sad to compound their grief and angst with a will that does not represent your current desires or promises to your family. Not to mention, the state of your will and planning can have an enormous impact on your estate's tax liability.

23. **Do you know what you want to do the day after you sell the business or retire?**

This is a bigger question than you might imagine. Many baby boomers will defer retirement or full retirement for a number of years. However, when owners sell, the likelihood of their being on for very long after the sale seems to be fairly low. Once your out, what will you do? Will you want to work for one or more nonprofits? Get attached now, while you are active and attractive. Want to do something for your church? Work with the pastor or administrator to get it defined before you are ready and you can work into it. Want to do something fun in a non-competing business? You might want to get something started now. Whatever it is you want to do, it is best to be thinking now about it and positioning yourself so that you can walk into that next portion of your life. If not you may find yourself bored and unemployed. That's not healthy.

24. **Who are your trusted advisers who are assisting you with your will, your gift and estate tax planning, your succession planning, retirement planning, your buy-sell agreement, and so on?**

Do you have a team? Is there a quarterback for the team? Does your family know the team? Are you working with them on an ongoing basis to assure that your management and ownership transitions will go smoothly and that your estate tax planning and "life after work" plans are well underway? If not, it is probably time to get started.

25. **Are you comfortable with the state of your planning for your future and the future of your family? Or are you vaguely or specifically uncomfortable with the state of your affairs?**

    If you are vaguely or specifically uncomfortable, now is the time to take action. If you are comfortable, chances are that you are already working with a professional team – either that or you are oblivious to the issues or hoping they don't apply to you! They do.

The 26th question is a bonus:

How can anyone answer the first 25 questions or get others to help answer them? The answer lies in making one simple decision – *employ The One Percent Solution and treat your investments in closely held businesses as the important investments they are.*

You will run your business. That is a fact. The question is whether you you manage the private company wealth you are creating, or can potentially create, with the same concern and respect that you manage your liquid wealth?

The answer to this question will determine, in large measure, how much liquid wealth you and your fellow owners will ultimately have. Start the process of managing your private company wealth today.

Epilogue

Remember Norm from the beginning of the book? Norm was real, but he is also a symbolic representation of many business owners in that he put off doing many important things for far too long. In the process, he put his family and future at risk.

Norm and I did get together. Over a several year period, Norm accomplished a number of objectives.

- Hired an experienced COO to help develop his sons as managers.

- Engaged in a leveraged buy-back transaction that generated $10 million of liquid wealth outside the business. The debt from that transaction has long been paid off.

- Instituted a regular dividend.

- Upgraded the company's operating systems to provide better inventory controls over multiple locations and better customer information.

- Survived the Great Recession.

Norm's business is far more ready for sale than when Nick visited him years ago. His wife is content that they have enough assets for her to live should anything happen to Norm. The sons are running the business.

And yes, Norm paid off the bass boat loan. And he bought a bigger boat for recreation and social use – and paid cash.

About the Author

Chris Mercer is the founder and CEO of Mercer Capital, one of the leading business appraisal firms in the nation. Chris has been valuing businesses and working with business owners for more than 30 years

Chris calls himself a businessman and a valuation guy. As a businessman, he has written more practical titles like *Buy-Sell Agreements for Closely Held and Family Business Owners* and *The One Percent Solution: An Introduction for Wealth Managers and Business Owners to the Concept of Managing Pre-Liquid Wealth*. From a valuation standpoint, he has written leading theoretical books like *Business Valuation: An Integrated Theory* and *Quantifying Marketability Discounts*.

Chris has served on the boards of several closely held and family businesses, on the board of one public company, and on the boards of several non-profit organizations. This book reflects a number of his experiences as a board member addressing issues like ownership and management transitions, leveraged dividend and leveraged stock buy-back transactions, and more.

Chris has been focused on ownership and management transitions for a long time, beginning with Mercer Capital. An ESOP was formed in 2006 to acquire about half of Mercer Capital's stock. Management was transitioned to the next generation who took over management in 2009. Ownership transitioning is continuing.

Chris speaks frequently to business owners and their advisers, increasingly focusing on issues facing baby boomer business owners in the midst of or facing critical management and ownership transitions at their companies.

Chris lives in Memphis, Tennessee, and spends time at his river house in Port Orange, Florida, whenever he can. He is a dedicated walker with a goal of walking at least 10,000 steps per day.

Public Speaking Engagements

Chris addresses topics related to managing private company wealth, ownership and management transitions, buy-sell agreements and valuation overview topics. Groups who have benefited from sessions include:

- Top-tier financial planners and insurance professionals dedicated to helping their clients with managing private company wealth

- Legal and accounting firms focused on building and maintaining relationships with owners of successful private businesses

- Industry associations dedicated to educating their members about private company wealth management and ownership and management transition issues

- Philanthropic organizations committed to educating business owner donors about benefits of using private company stock to achieve charitable goals

- Family offices

- Multi-firm family office firms dedicated to enhancing private company wealth management and encouraging the use of corporate finance tools to achieve liquidity and diversification for clients

Copies of *Unlocking Private Company Wealth* can be provided to attendees to add value to the events as part of the overall agreement.

For speaking fees and availability, contact Chris

mercerc@mercercapital.com

901-685-2120 (ask for Barbara Price or Chris Mercer)

Private Speaking Engagements

Chris can address your company's senior management and/or your board of directors in private meetings where interactive dialogue is desired. He will spend an appropriate amount of time in preparation for the meeting based on information you provide and will then come prepared to discuss valuation-related topics, ownership and management transition issues, and other identified issues that are agreed upon in advance. This is a tailored service.

Chris has spoken all over the United States and in a number of other countries, including Australia, Brazil, Hong Kong, Italy, Russia and others.

Call Chris directly to discuss availability and pricing at 901-579-9700.

Order More Copies of Unlocking Private Company Wealth

Do you know somebody who could benefit from reading *Unlocking Private Company Wealth*? It is the perfect gift for a friend, a relative, a fellow owner or a business adviser.

_____ copies @ $25.00 each = $ _____

(plus tax for TN and KY residents)
(plus shipping :: $5.00 for first book, $2.00 for each add'l)
(copies ship prepaid within one business day of receipt of order)

Full Name _____

Company _____

Mailing Address _____

City, State _____ Zip _____

Phone _____ Email _____

Check enclosed payable to Peabody Publishing, LP in the amount of: $ _____

To order via credit card: (Circle One)   Visa   Master Card   Amex

Credit Card # _____ Exp. Date _____

Name on Card _____

Signature _____

Mail or fax completed order form and payment to:
Peabody Publishing, LP
5100 Poplar Avenue, Suite 2600, Memphis, TN 38137
901.685.2120 (p) • 901.685.2199 (f)

To order online, visit
www.ChrisMercer.net/books
www.MercerCapital.com